A Parenting Toolkit

Raising Emotionally Healthy and Socially Competent Children

ANNE K. SODERMAN

Table of Contents

Dedicated with love to

Michael, John, Randi, and Alexander.

Preface

Rarely will you find two people who marry or partner together who agree on everything. Often, in fact, we are first attracted to and remain interested in people who complement rather than mirror us, who have at least some characteristics different than ours. Where parenting is concerned, however, we need to find common ground and proven practice—and the earlier, the better. It makes the whole job easier, and our children are more likely to turn out as pretty nice human beings if we do. After all, that's our ultimate goal, as well as being able to enjoy them while they're growing into adolescence and beyond.

In a perfect world, people who are thinking about becoming parents would acknowledge the seriousness of what they are about to do. They would evaluate the timing and financial aspects of having children and take at least minimal training in how to be an effective parent. They would find out how they differ with one another on their approach to parenting *before* they become parents. In the real world, as we all know, that rarely happens.

Instead, more often than not, children just come along -- planned or unplanned, and many people simply grow into their parenting on a day-to-day, discovery-mode basis. Sometimes it works out okay, and sometimes it doesn't. Ironically, there's probably nothing else that will consume as much of our time, emotion, and finances over a lifetime – for good or for ill.

There's plenty of evidence around us about cause and effect in parenting. We see people who raise likeable, capable children and those who don't. We see children who function well both inside and outside of their family circles and others who have enormous problems in handling their emotions, self-regulation, interactions with others, and making choices about healthy behaviors.

Sometimes, it's just one child in the family who seems troubled or one who makes it against all odds.

Most of the parenting books already on the market today focus almost exclusively on discipline strategies – how to get children to do what we want them to do. The problem is, that's not all there is to raising emotionally healthy and socially competent children. Also, kids are smarter than that. Eventually, they catch on to being "techniqued." They don't like it and usually resist it. In the decades of work that my colleagues and I have done with parents and teachers in child development, and the textbooks we have written to prepare teachers to work successfully with children, we know that simply having a bag full of tricks to direct or correct a child's behavior accomplishes little related to the more important, long-range outcomes we need to shoot for.

This book has been written for those of you with children 2-12 years of age. Its purpose is to share the best of what is known currently about effective parenting. I've tried to distill this down so that I don't put you to sleep as a reader but not so much that I leave you without the research-based tools you need.

I'm confident that the six most important principles for parenting that are described in Chapter 1 will hold true as you're navigating through developmental changes in your children and family over time – even some tough ones. In Chapter 2, the book centers on how emotional intelligence develops, effects of temperament, and how you can build resilience and stress hardiness in your children. Chapter 3 is all about helping children expand their social environments in an increasingly complex world. That's when outside influences and technology will begin to take on additional weight. Then, because a child may come along with special developmental needs or meet others who have them, Chapter 4 is centered on better understanding and supporting exceptionalities. Finally, because of the prevalence of divorce in our society today, I felt compelled to add Chapter 5. It takes an in-depth look at helping children cope with family restructuring if that should happen.

Over time, there have been common questions that parents have asked about certain areas of development or discipline, and several are included in each chapter. Also, no matter how good our foundation is for understanding development or our consistency in sticking to best practices, things will not always move along perfectly. Children are active in their own development, and parents occasionally experience bumps in the road that throw them off track temporarily. In each chapter, I've pointed out a few possibilities to watch out for and have labeled them *Red Flags*. A concluding section in each chapter, called *What's in Your Parenting Toolkit?* will remind you of the dependable tools you have to deal with unexpected setbacks and to keep you on the road to good, solid parenting. For those of you who would like to read further about child development and ways to create healthy environments for growing children, refer to the research-based notes/reference listing by chapter at the end of the book.

Being a parent should always be hopeful, *mostly* predictable, and ultimately gratifying. As the mother of three very fine adult children, I can honestly say that my trip has never been boring, and yours won't be, either.

CHAPTER 1

Parenting That Has Staying Power

I don't have to tell you that the world in which you grew up is very different than the one in which you're raising your children. Your parents could never have imagined that we would have cars that drive and park themselves, I-phones and an internet that can reach anywhere in the world in seconds, or printers that can turn out a chess set or a pair of shoes. They weren't worried about climate change, a virus that could shut down the entire world, or global markets. Still, they wanted the same thing for you that you want for your own children—that you would grow up emotionally healthy and socially competent. That hasn't changed.

While I can't predict what the world will be like in another 20 years for today's three-year-old, I am certain there are 6 parenting practices that, if used consistently, can definitely increase the chances that your children will better understand themselves and respect others. As they grow, there will be a greater probability that they'll devclop the self-regulation, resilience, and pro-social behaviors that are common in healthy adolescents and adults and that you want to see in them.

Life inside a family doesn't always unfold the way we envisioned before forming our own families. It's definitely never as predictable as we would like, and every family will experience some "ups and downs." That's true about parenting as well. Spouses may find themselves in a power struggle with one another over the best way to handle a child's challenging behavior. One parent could be worried that the other one is not always a positive role model in terms of handling day-to-day pressure or is a poor disciplinarian— sometimes too harsh or too soft. A child may come along with special needs that will make parenting more difficult. Or, over time, there may be major transitions such as divorce and remarriage that no one planned on.

When parenting or family life seems to be tougher than usual or more stressful than it should be, examine how well you've been relying on the following six principles:

Parenting Principle #1:
Build self-regulation in your children by being an authoritative parent.

There are four very distinct discipline styles or approaches to parenting: *authoritarian, permissive, uninvolved, and authoritative.*[1] Some of the characteristics of each particular style can be seen in Figure 1 below and are also reflected in each of the four families described. As you consider these examples, think about your own style and which quadrant you'd fall into.

Parenting Styles

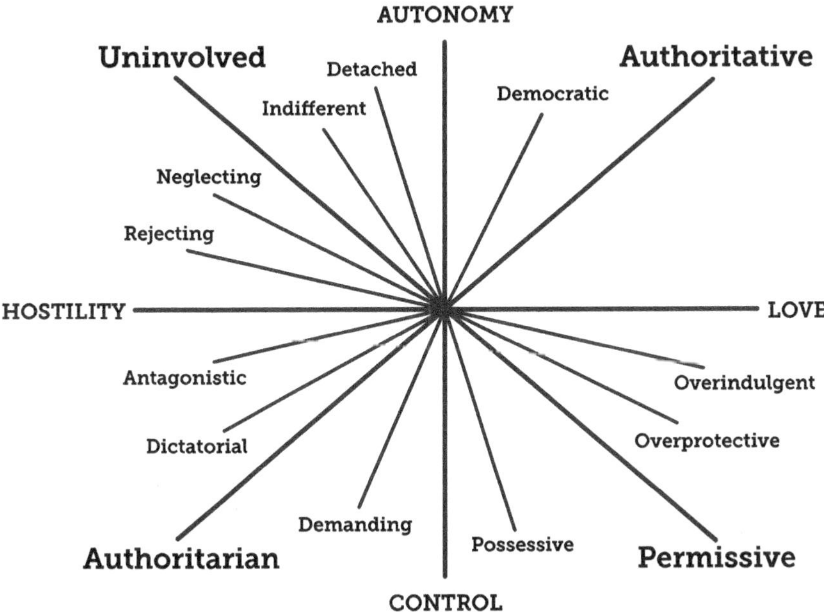

Figure 1. Parenting styles—Authoritarian, Permissive, Uninvolved, and Authoritative.

Consider these parents. Watch for whether or not they *set clear expectations* for their children, the *extent to which they communicate* those, and the *degree to which they are likely to enforce compliance* when they ask their children to do something If you were a child in one of these families, would you feel cared about and valued?[2]

Victor and Leah have two children, ages 7 and 10. They frequently argue over how to handle their two boys. "Leah is way too protective and most of the time, they get away with murder," says Victor. "They have to grow up some time! She's making sissies out of them."

"Victor thinks I'm too soft on the boys," counters Leah. "Just because his parents were abusive doesn't mean we have to be. They're afraid of him!"

Bill and Marilyn: "I guess you could describe us as fairly hands-off parents," muses Bill. "Marilyn works long hours, and I'm definitely not able to be home very much. We've got good kids—well, most of the time, I guess. My mom and dad think they're growing up like weeds and don't get enough of our attention, but what're you going to do? We deserve a life, too!"

Kendra and Alex: "All in all, I think we're doing pretty well with our three. We expect a lot, and they measure up pretty well—so far, so good. We definitely don't spoil them, but when an issue comes up, we try to reason it through with them or talk about what else they could have done. In the end, though, we still make the hard decisions. I'm just thankful Alex and I are on the same page with each other."

Jeremy and Elaine: "There's no question that we're way too easy on our kids. We didn't have the best time growing up, so I guess Elaine and I want them to have everything we didn't. Her parents were super critical (still are!), and mine home schooled us so that we wouldn't run into any "bad influences." We don't have TV in our home for the same reason. We do know the kids play all those sketchy video games at a neighbor's house, but we've never said anything to them about it. We probably should. We just want our kids to know that we love them, so I admit that we don't make a lot of demands on them.

Obviously, parents sometimes disagree with one another about which style is best for rearing their children. They may also feel most comfortable disciplining their children with strategies their *own* parents used, even if they resented them while growing up. Some may allow their emotions to dictate how they respond to their children at any particular time.

Getting into a routine of parenting in the authoritarian, permissive, or uninvolved quadrants in Figure 1 spells trouble for the future of a child. In the authoritarian approach, parents are harsh and often distant, inclined to value unquestioning obedience above all else. They view reasoning and explanations as wholly unnecessary and not part of the "rule book" or at least not part of *their* rule book. They're inclined to deal with broken rules as flaunting their authority and as justification for swift punishment. That might involve corporal punishment such as hitting or name calling, shaming, and labeling ("You sound just like your father!" "You're just a liar…a brat…lazy…stupid…no good!" "I can never depend on you, can I?"). As they grow older, these children frequently look for someone smaller or weaker to bully. They usually have trouble seeing others' perspectives or being empathic and are more likely to act out when they feel no one is looking.

Permissive parents are quite the opposite. While they love their children and are turned off by physical punishment and blind obedience, they create very few boundaries for their children. Most of all, they fear the loss of their children's love and affection, leading them to accept behavior they shouldn't. Some of these parents are inclined to use a technique called "love withdrawal" when their children have been disrespectful or hurtful to others, telling their children, "I won't love you if you act like that." or "Nice children don't do that." Besides those unkind statements, however, they seldom make demands that their children change their behavior in a more positive direction; rarely do they administer any penalties for transgressions. This leaves children with little awareness of how their uncontrolled behavior affects others. Their inability to connect cause and effect, lack of empathy for others, and no-holds-barred behavior often result in a lack of friendships with other children, as well as disapproval by other adults. The long-range outcome is usually low self-esteem and poor school performance.

Uninvolved parents also provide little guidance to their children and seem almost indifferent to what goes on. As long as they aren't personally bothered, these detached and narcissistic adults expend little energy on their children. Compounding this approach is the fact that parents in the uninvolved quadrant also express little affection for their children—which does not bode well for the future. The result is that as these children grow older, they tend to be non-compliant, irresponsible, and immature. The likelihood is great for poor academic performance, truancy, delinquency, drug use and precocious sexuality.

Authoritative parents play in an entirely different arena. They traditionally use higher levels of communication with their children, are affectionate, make reasonable maturity demands, and exercise control that changes as their children grow older and are able to behave more independently and responsibly. They help them understand that their discipline and redirection are targeted at teaching them how to behave, not as punishment. They use wrong-doing as opportunities to develop consciousness about others, alternative possibilities for next time, and on-the-spot coaching.

These children are fairly easy to spot. For the most part, they are cooperative, happy, high achievers, friendly, and helpful to others. While it may sound as if they live in families that resemble the doo-wop families of the 1950s, their parents aren't pushovers. When issues are difficult to resolve to everyone's satisfaction, parent control always trumps the child exerting control. These parents are in the driver's seat, and they want their children to know that!

In electing to parent this way, you have to pay attention to how you communicate your expectations when you're redirecting your child's behavior. Do you launch right into what they're doing wrong, using words such as *never* or *always* and commands ("You never put your bike away. I've told you a million times. Do it!")? If so, here's what is sure to work better: Try using a *personal message* to let them know how their behavior is affecting you (or someone else) and why the behavior is unsafe, destructive, or infringing on someone else.

Using personal messages may not come naturally to you. It didn't to me when I first learned about the value in using them and began to try them out. Because of that, I want to emphasize here that it takes commitment to replacing less effective communication with them and practicing until it becomes effortless—but it's worth it! Following are the steps in delivering a personal message:

1. Use a reflection to state the behavior you've seen, considering your child's point of view (ex. "You were in a hurry to get inside and left your bike in the driveway.").

2. Describe your emotions and the reason for them ("It's upsetting when you do that. I'm worried I might drive over it.").

3. State the behavior you want now, as well as in the future ("Put your bike in the garage where it belongs."). This is a very clear statement of what you want instead of the behavior you've just seen.

Personal messages are not only used for moving behavior in another direction. You will also want to use them to provide genuine compliments for a job well done or when your child exhibits growing responsibility. You do that by using only the first two steps and eliminating the third part of the message:

"Hey, you shoveled the walk without even being asked. That saves me a big job, and I'm grateful. Thanks."

"You helped your mother clear the dishwasher. I was happy to see that."

"You love playing that piece on the piano. I really enjoy listening to it!"

Personal messages are more effective than overused phrases such as "Good job!" "Way to go!" or "You're just a great kid!" that are non-specific and don't say anything about *why* you're pleased; as such, they are less likely to reinforce a child's positive behavior—and you're less likely to see it again. These two-part personal messages let your child know *specifically* the kinds of behaviors that please you or others and make them feel pleased to hear it; consequently, they're more likely to repeat it in the future.

Now for the important part. What do you do when your child ignores what you've asked him to do? It's frustrating, and you may be tempted to deep-six authoritative parenting in favor of another style that could have awful long-range outcomes but immediate action on the part of the child. Keep your cool. Remember that you can get what you want and still keep your relationship with your child a positive one. Here's where you apply corrective consequences. They can be natural, logical, or unrelated. For example, let's use the example where you've asked your child to put his bike in the garage after using it so you don't run over it.

You could use a *natural consequence* and take the chance of running over it. If that happened, it would be important not to replace the bike and just let the child go without it. However, in this case, that doesn't seem reasonable, does it? So, you reject that as a corrective consequence and move to the next possibility of using a *logical consequence*. If you see the bike in the driveway again, you tell him, "You've left your bike in the driveway again. You can either put it in the garage right now and in the future without being asked or you'll lose the privilege of using it for a week." Notice that you've used an "*either/or*" sequence. You start by using a reflection (naming the specific behavior) and then telling the child what will happen if he doesn't comply. You say this calmly and then you get busy doing something and give him several minutes to do what you've asked. You do not forget to follow up. You do **not** count (1….2….3….) while you're waiting (PLEASE don't do that!). You do **not** give another warning, not even one more. Don't moralize or judge. Be quiet. Then, if nothing happens or you see that darned bike in the driveway again in the future, you tell your child, "You chose to leave your bike in the driveway. Remember I told you to either put it in the garage or you would lose the privilege of using it for a week. Now, go put it in the garage and leave it there for the week." I like to use the words "You chose…" when having to use a corrective consequence. It reminds the child that the decision *not* to comply was all his. If he begs to have you let him use the bike before the week is up and won't stop, implement a subsequent warning ("You want to argue over this. You can either stop or it'll be another week."). If you stick to your guns, when your child hears the "either/or" sequence, he'll know you mean business, that he has a chance to correct his behavior or that he can rely on your following through with the consequence. It doesn't change.

Whenever possible, use natural or logical corrective consequences. Unrelated consequences should only be used as a last resort because they don't have lasting value in developing the child's internalization of the behaviors that are important to you. For example, you could have told your son that if you see the bike in the driveway again, there won't be any TV for a week. That makes less sense in that one has nothing to do with the other, and the consequence takes the form of a punishment instead. Corrective consequences should be instructive, teach a child how to correct mistaken behavior, give the child a chance to correct it, be reasonable, and focus on a change for the future. Punishments, on the other hand, are not instructive, are not related to the behavior, are concentrated on retaliation, and applied with disrespect or indifference by the adult. They produce resentment in a child.

Exercising authoritative parenting is one of the most important elements in raising a healthy, self-regulated child. This doesn't happen all at once and evolves gradually, progressing from no sense of right or wrong in a very young child to responding to various rewards and/or punishments. As they grow older, children adopt certain codes of behavior in order to please or be like someone they admire. This eventually propels them toward developing the standards and ideals that will become important to them in adulthood.

The most advanced form of self-regulation is when your children's behavior is truly an extension of their own internalized beliefs about how people should act and what they believe about larger moral concepts. When those have become strongly centered principles in terms of justice, honesty and equity, children will treat others well and behave well, not because someone is watching them or telling them to do so. It will be because they have developed an internal guide that helps them *choose* to behave in terms of their own internalized values and ethics. These frequently match the beliefs of their parents or other models that have become important to them. They can be positive or negative, depending on what children have witnessed most often in terms of prosocial or antisocial consequences. If you are interested in learning more about the benefits of authoritative parenting and the implementation of skills, read further in Kostelnik et al., *Guiding Children's Development and Learning*.[3]

Parenting Principle #2:
Be Consistent.

Consider what these parents say:

Bruce: "Molly, our 4-year old, never quite knows what her mother is going to be like when she gets up in the morning. Nancy's definitely what I'd call a "mood mother." If she's feeling good, Molly can get away with almost anything. If she's worried or upset about something, she has a very short fuse. It's definitely getting to be a problem, not only for our daughter but for me. I've just about had it!"

Jia and Merrill are parents of three children, 8-year-old twin boys and a 4-year-old daughter. Pretty much in agreement about the way they approach their parenting, they believe their children need explanations for behavior requests. However, when the children step outside their established family guidelines for behavior, they back one another in what should happen. "Our kids don't always like it," laughs Jia, "but they know we're fair and we aren't going to fold under pressure."

Emily: I remember learning very quickly that when my mother told us to do something that we were fully able to do, she was not going to nag or keep reminding us; but she was also not going to let us get away with not doing it—not ever. My dad was a different story, though. He could be 'wheedled,' and we all knew it. It used to drive my mother crazy."

Growing up isn't always the piece of cake many adults think it is. We forget a lot between childhood and adulthood but tend to remember how it was in terms of "being" in our own particular families. Children have a big job in terms of learning how to adapt to what's expected of them year after year, both at home and in school. It helps when they can count on family life being consistent in terms of parental values and daily routines and if parents are on the same page with one another about values and routines.

In the last section, we described an authoritative approach to discipline. Consistency plays a critical part in carrying it off well. When it's absent, a sense of insecurity can pervade childhood, as well as discouragement and self-doubt. When parents are unpredictable, children can become manipulative, particularly when they discover that one parent does not support the other. Such children learn that a good mood signals the time to ask for something and a bad mood signals a time to avoid that parent. If being aggressive toward a sibling is ignored by one parent but not the other, there's a good chance that the child will continue to be aggressive but simply get more cautious about doing it, depending on who's watching. It all gets very confusing.

It's expected that parenting routines will change a bit over time, depending on the age of the child and activity with the family, but these changes should be gradual rather than dramatic. For example, when children have a consistent bedtime and bedtime rituals, there is often less struggle in getting them to bed in the evening. As they get older, bedtime may come later, but there is still the understanding that when it's time to go to bed, there shouldn't be an argument over it, that teeth need to be brushed before going to bed, and that people say goodnight to one another before going off to bed. When mealtimes are regular, children with consistent routines know that they are expected to be home on time, help with preparation of the meal or setting of the table, and cleaning up. As children enter elementary school, homework becomes a predictable part of the picture and when parents hold the line and communicate effectively about when and where it is to be completed, children develop the self-regulation that is needed to take care of the job without constant oversight on the part of parents. They know what is expected of them, that it's their job to take care of it, and that it will be easier to do so than not to.

Families also develop habits and routines with respect to such leisure-time activities as TV viewing and use of other devices. Ten-year-old Virgil understands that he can make certain choices about what to watch on TV but that he only gets two hours a day. This doesn't change from day to day or week to week. He also understands that he is only allowed to use the computer in the kitchen and that videos and Apps are counted as part of the media allotment. Occasionally, he whines that "all the other kids" he knows can watch all the TV or play all the Apps they want. Internally, however, he knows that his mother will respond the way she always does with her predictable line, "That may be." He has come to understand the few "rules" that are part of the Bernero family's way of doing business.

Being consistent does not mean that parents are completely inflexible or intractable about what goes on. For example, when Juno began playing soccer after school, the family's regular dinner hour was moved from 6:00 to 7:00 to accommodate his practice schedule. What was not changed was the importance of the family sitting down together for the evening meal. Homework that had usually been done following a snack after school was moved to after dinner. What was not changed was the definition of a particular time for completion of that task.

Parenting Principle #3:
Spend Focused Time.

Consider these parents:

Ian and Jennifer have 5 children. "How in the world have you had time to raise such great children?" asks their next-door neighbor. "We have two, and it's a full-time job!" "Thanks," says Jennifer, "but we made up our mind when the third one came along that we were going to spend at least 5 minutes a day focused completely on each one of our children and what *they* were interested in. That's not a lot of time, but I think it's been important."

Cameron and Susan were married for 8 years and divorced when their children were 4, 6, and 10, deciding that it "just wasn't going to get any better." Susan has since remarried and moved to another state. According to Cameron, Susan works hard to alienate the children against him, despite the fact that he wants to be a significant part of their lives. "She tells the children before they leave for their 'visitations' with me how much their friends will miss them and how difficult it is for her to 'let them go.' It takes them a long time to warm up on a visit, and I'm worried things are only going to get worse in the future if she keeps this up. She refuses to even consider letting me have them for an extra couple of days or for special events in my family that don't coincide with the court-granted dates. She acts like she's doing me a favor to let me see my own kids!"

Remember Harry Chapin's sad little song, *Cat's in the Cradle*, made popular by Bob Seeger and Eric Clapton? It begins, "My child arrived just the other day. He came to the world in the usual way. But there were planes to catch and bills to pay. He learned to walk while I was away. And he was talkin' 'fore I knew it, and as he grew, he'd say, I'm gonna be like you, Dad. You know I'm gonna be like you."

As it turns out, there were always things that got in the way of their spending any decent time with one another and when the now-retired father asks his adult son when they're going to get together, the son responds, "I'd love to, Dad, if I can find the time. You see….my new job's a hassle and the kids……" In the remaining verses, the father is hit hard with the fact that, indeed, his son has grown up to be just like him, with good intentions but no time to follow through to be with one another.[4] Somehow, "life" just kept getting in the way.

There have been a lot of studies about what teen-agers wish were different in their relationship with their parents as they were growing up. This may be surprising, but most say they wished their parents had spent more time with them and that many of them miss the closeness they once had with their parents when they were very little.

When children are still preschoolers, parents are likely to spend large amounts of time taking care of their physical needs but also involved in their leisure time activities, bedtime routines, modeling and discussing behavior, and interacting with their child's teachers. What happens to that as children move into the primary years and toward adolescence?

It's natural that as children grow older, they will move increasingly out of the family circle and begin to interact more with peers and other adults, both on a formal and informal basis. However, children still need and hope for guidance, affection, and attention from their parents as they increase their independence.

Also, as additional children come along, children in a family sometimes lose any individuality with respect to having time alone with their parents. Stephen remembers:

"We were always just 'THE KIDS.' After a certain age, I don't remember that we did anything separately with either one of our parents unless it was something like going to the doctor. They never had time to come to any of my games and even birthdays weren't special. I remember that my mom would always say, 'So, what do you kids want to do to celebrate Stephen's birthday?' What about just asking *me* what I wanted to do to celebrate my birthday?"

Marvin McKinney, one of 6 siblings who turned out to be highly successful in business, education and medicine, grew up in a low-income black neighborhood in Detroit, Michigan.

"When my mom died, we went back for the funeral," he noted. "We were all sitting around the kitchen table with my dad and sharing our memories about Mom. I happened to say, 'You know, we never had two dimes to rub together, but I remember Mom slipping me a nickel every now and then, giving me a big hug, and telling me how special I was—and I grew up thinking I *was* pretty special.' My sister laughed, and when I asked her what she was laughing about, she said, 'Marv, Mom did that with all of us kids! Each one of us thought we were the favored one. As it turns out, we all were—at one time or another."[5]

Scheduled vacations create future memories for parents and children, even when things don't always go as planned. That is a time for families to suspend all of the usual activities, friends, and responsibilities that take them away from one another on a day-to-day basis and to spend focused time with one another. As children grow older and get involved with sports and other commitments, and parents become more entrenched with job responsibilities, a common time to take a vacation becomes more difficult. However, it's worth it to try and figure out to steadfastly work at least a week or long weekend in for a family holiday with one another.

Vacations help bind family members together in terms of looking forward to a future event together and building "remember when…." escapades with one another. In close families, these scenes are played over and over, with special meaning only to the family members that participated in those special times with one another.

Don't fall for that old "quality time" versus "quantity of time" thing. Kids need both. One of the most important messages you can send your child is, "I value you enough to choose to spend time with you as opposed to always spending it with other people and doing other things." Accept that there may never be the "perfect" moment, and make the best of the five-, ten-, or fifteen-minute opportunities you get as they come. Don't put your child off throughout the day thinking you're getting other obligations out of the way so you can devote two hours to the ball game or the big dinner out. Children need consistent, continuous contact time with both parents.

Parenting Principle #4:
Provide for Needs Rather than Wants.

Consider these parents:

Henry: "I grew up with nothing…nada! And it was miserable. I was ashamed in school because I never had the right clothes. Everyone knew I got free lunch, that my dad didn't have a decent job, and that we lived on the wrong side of the tracks. That's not going to happen to my kids. I work hard to make sure it won't, and I'm proud that they're getting the best of everything.

Consuella and Juan: "Our kids know that when we take them to the store that they're not going to get something new every time and that they need to save up for what they want except for birthdays and holidays. That's when we buy something special, but that's not an everyday occurrence. That's for sure."

In the above example, Henry may believe he is providing the "best of everything" for his children, but children who have nothing to work for or receive all they want with very little effort are likely missing something very important that they need developmentally. Children must learn to delay gratification, to learn to wait, and learn to work for what is important to them. Delayed gratification is one of the most important components in emotional intelligence. It can be a difficult concept for children to grasp—and even harder to embrace and value—if there is no modeling to do so.

Children who don't learn how to delay gratification are more likely to have poor impulse control in the future, and they often demonstrate less respect for others. Obviously, delayed gratification is definitely not something that is easy to learn or to exercise. Usually, two different parts of our brain are in contention at the same time in situations where we are attracted to something. For example, many of us are motivated to lose weight, but we can't resist that extra dessert. As a nation, we know intellectually that we shouldn't buy things we can't afford but tend to overuse and even abuse credit. Too often, our emotional brain wins out, even though we fully understand that there are consequences to an overloaded credit card and an overloaded mid-section.

David Elkind, well-known child psychologist, remembers that when he was little, he wanted a Captain Marvel ring more than anything in the world. He said that he never let up on his mother for a period of time about that ring, saying, "I want it. I just want it. I'll never ask for anything else, ever. I *need* it, Mom." He still remembers her looking at him and saying, "David, you may want it, but you don't *need* it. There's a big difference. Save your money if you want it."[6]

Even if we could afford to give our children everything they want, we shouldn't. And that takes our disciplining ourselves about the way we model needs and wants with our children. If we buy everything *we* want or never demonstrate limiting ourselves about anything, it becomes very difficult to say to children, "You want it, but you don't *need* it." Look for opportunities to demonstrate delayed gratification so that children understand the concept. We don't have to moralize about it or to sound like a martyr about what we're doing, but it helps children if adults involve them in some actual reflection and thought about how we make decisions between our own wants and needs. For example, "We could put that new TV set (computer, phone….) on a credit card, but we don't really need it. We just want it. If we save $100 a month (for X months), we can just pay cash for it. Let's do it that way!" or "An ice cream cone would really taste good right now, but it would spoil our dinner since it's already 4:30. Let's make a healthier choice and wait until Saturday when we're back in town again and can time it better."

As your children are growing, constantly help them monitor their needs and wants. What they *need* is access to good health care and nutrition, exercise, growing ability to make and maintain friendships, rest and sleep, learning how to make good decisions and solve problems, and time with immediate and extended family members. They need to value others and obtain a solid education that will help them eventually find meaningful work and become financially independent. Everything else is gravy, and too much gravy can be unhealthy.

Parenting Principle #5:
Create and Maintain a Climate of Respect and Harmony.

Consider what these parents say:

Elsa: "Any parent will tell you that when you take on the responsibility of raising a child, it comes with the free gift of anxiety in all its forms, intermittent exhaustion, and often reality-altering love and devotion."

Gilbert: "Sometimes I come home, and Ellen is frazzled with the kids. I'm always tempted to tell her, 'They'll be grown up before we know it. Enjoy this time with them!' On the other hand, I realize that she's carrying a lot more of the load with the kids right now, and the best thing I could say is 'Let me take them right now. You need a break.'"

Audrey: "I remember that when I was a child, my whole world would be upside down when my parents argued with one another, and life was really good when they demonstrated their love for one another. My insecurity barometer would go sky high when things weren't going well, and that was most of the time. I don't know that they recognized what a profound effect their moods and treatment of one another had on us kids."

Inside a family, there are two elements that can be extremely harmful to children's development: disrespect between family members and undue, ongoing amounts of stress. While children are resilient, there's good evidence that cognitive development, self-esteem, and psychological well-being are negatively affected in families characterized by disrespect and/or high levels of stress.

Disrespect can show up in families in a number of different ways, but the result is always increased stress, resentment, and distancing of members. It evolves from the following:

- Lack of effective communication and support between parents
- Hostile and destructive behavior between family members
- Chaotic or disconnected lifestyles

Lack of Effective Communication and Support between Parents

Those "ups and downs" that we mentioned earlier that are common to most families may include any of the following: members coming into or leaving the family; physical or mental health issues; job-related stresses (too much work; not making a promotion; loss of a job; stress with co-workers); moving location; spousal sexual or intimacy problems; and arguments over housework, handling money, and raising the children.

What would you say if I told you that someone could predict with 90 percent accuracy whether your marriage would succeed or fail—by just watching how you talk with one another about issues, your body language as the other person is talking, and the way you handle controversy about challenges that come your way? After decades of laboratory research, psychologists John M. Gottman and his colleagues have demonstrated the ability to do just that. They have listened to couples that tell them, "We don't feel close anymore." "He never talks to me." "He only has time for the kids." "All she does is work." Their conclusions may not be complex, but they are highly predictable: Couples who stay together happily behave like good friends. They handle their conflicts in gentle, positive ways. Those who don't make it have observable problems with criticism, blaming, defensiveness, showing contempt for one another (sarcasm, mocking, name calling, belligerence) and stonewalling or withdrawing from one another when in disagreement.[7]

While there can be cultural differences in the way family members interact with one another, there is much more harmony in any family when parents talk with one another and come to agreement about the way they will spend money, where they will live, the values that are important to them, how they will raise their children, issues related to religious practices, education, sexual intimacy, and the intersection between work and family. Those are the big areas for mutual decision-making, and it may seem obvious that spouses or partners should talk with one another about those things. But—some don't.

There is also day-to-day communication that's needed where family members check in with one another and where parents share the challenges that arise in daily life when working, partnering, and raising children together. That includes both the satisfactions and dissatisfactions. The way that you connect with one another will create the emotional climate in which you will raise your children. It should be no surprise that a spousal relationship that includes empathy for one another, affection, and respectful ways of interacting sets the tone for a stable family life. Unfortunately, unresolved anger and resentment also create a tone.

Hostile Behavior

When parents or children openly argue or fight with one another, say cutting things to one another, or engage in cold wars, everyone is made uncomfortable or damaged. When parents are openly at odds with one another, children feel out of control. No matter their age, they worry when they see their parents losing control with one another and eventually lose respect for an abusive parent, as well as for the parent who is being abused. They learn to fear the out-of-control parent and can develop avoidant behavior or guilt if they are unable to protect a parent or sibling who might be the current target of that person's rage. Worst of all, they may learn to be abusive themselves, watching the misuse of power in terms of coercing others and coming to think that it works to get what one wants.

Disrespect by children toward one another or toward parents is also problematic in a family when parents allow it. For example, in the Mahler family, there is a definite pecking order that has developed among the three children. Sibling rivalry is intense, and Mrs. Mahler frequently gets involved by siding with one child over another or punishing everyone when she's "had enough." Resentment in this family is alive and well, but little is being learned about caring ways to behave with one another, how to settle conflicts without inappropriate power, or how to compromise. That's not good for the Mahler children or the families they will create in the future. For example, 4-year-old Jia frequently throws temper tantrums in the store when she picks out something she wants and is told no by her mother or father. Instead of gathering her up and heading for the car, they more often cave in and buy it for her, thereby reinforcing her behavior for next time. Her mother believes she will eventually grow out of this behavior, but Jia is learning some very important lessons for the future in terms of how she will interact with them and with others. Jia is becoming an emotional bully.

Chaotic or Disconnected Lifestyles

Where there is undue stress, there's an absence of harmony. Today's western lifestyles are often an invitation for marital and parenting disaster. Both children and parents can become heavily overscheduled in terms of non-family activity, particularly after children enter formal schooling. Everyone is going in a different direction, and homes become more of a stopping off place to rest and refuel, but little else.

Some families take control of this, making a commitment to spend time together within the family and to eliminate the constant coming and going that characterizes many families and which results in tremendous stress. For example, Bob has been offered a different position as school principal in another state. It means a promotion, a larger school to manage, and potentially more "advantages" to his three children than are available in the small rural town in which they are living. After talking it over, he and his wife have decided that the change would be too disruptive to their family life. It would mean longer working hours and more time away from home. They realize that some of the things they have come to value in that small rural town for their children and themselves are important to them as a family. Much to the distress of his highly ambitious parents, Bob has declined the job offer, noting that if he does a good job where he is, he should have other opportunities. In another family, the parents monitor the number of extra-curricular activities in which their children are involved after school and on the weekends, wanting them to be thoughtful about those they choose to do.

Stress is neither good nor bad. It almost always results from too much or too little of something—too much change, too much activity, and too much ambiguity or uncertainty or too little stimulation, too few resources, or too little security. It can result from the absence of any predictable routine in a family, so that children feel there is little order in their world. The younger children are, the more these feelings are likely to emerge. The failure to develop and maintain routines gets in the way of their learning to manage impulsive behavior, curbs self-discipline, and removes the secure anchor children need to guarantee a sense of security.

Parenting Principle #6:
Cultivate and Preserve a Family Identity

Consider these parents:

Kim and Hal: "Joy is only 3, but we've lived in three different countries with her. The current school has a terrific parent website with pictures of her in her preschool class, and her grandparents in Boston and Wilmington check in on that every week—probably every day—to see how she's doing. We get home to each of our families twice a year. That's important. We want her to know her cousins, aunts, uncles, and grandparents—even if she is a world traveler."

Marian: "I don't let Castor see his paternal grandparents at all. They never liked me when I was married to their son, and they'd just bad-mouth me. I don't need that, and neither does Castor!"

In our family, it wouldn't be Christmas Eve without Swedish potato sausage, and even though we tell the same stories over and over again, they still get the same laughs. As the younger children in the family were growing up, they looked forward to getting together with Uncle Mike and Aunt Randi and seeing their parents' first-grade pictures hanging on their grandparents' Christmas tree. Aunt Randi has lately become the social director in the family, taking on extra responsibility for getting family members all together at least once a year to catch up and enjoy one another. When Covid-19 limited traveling, she instituted a new ritual for the family—Zoom calls on one another's birthdays when face-to-face celebrations are not possible. During the holidays, there are games like *Boggle*, Spoons, and *Apples to Apples*, which get very competitive (but that's a lot of the fun!), and other rituals and quirks that exist in the Soderman family.

As in other families, these rituals promote a way to hang on to our family history. They contain humor and include meanings understood really well only by those in the family "circle." For us and for other families, they have built a caring sense of belonging to a meaningful group and have provided a valued family identity.

Every family develops some meaningful habits, customs, and practices that become traditional and unique to that family. There are some that don't necessarily serve as a bond to the extended family or with holidays that have become even more valuable because they are part of an immediate family tapestry. For example, Saturday morning is a time in the Cuthbert family when everyone pitches in to clean the house and then take a bike ride. Friday night, all three kids in the Tenant family hop up with their parents on their king-sized bed, share a big tub of popcorn, and watch a favorite show together. These are things that might not go on forever as the kids get older but long enough to build solid memories of good family times together.

You may have some family rituals that you don't even consider a ritual but will become extremely meaningful to your growing children—the bedtime story ritual when they were little, a special meal, the way you celebrate birthdays, a homemade birthday cake, family softball games where everyone participates as a fan or a player, or the annual summer garden with each person taking responsibility for one vegetable. Your family history will be knit together by the camping trips, the trips to Grandma and Grandpa's house, and the annual picture taking of that whole table of frosted sugar cookies. You will develop your own traditions, building them from those events that you do again and again that give special meaning and belonging. They will be the essential cement that holds your family together and gives it strength in the years to come.

As your children become older or your family is restructured through divorce and/or remarriage, are there new traditions or rituals that can be introduced? What can you do together that doesn't cost a lot of money or time? What kinds of family activities can you look forward to doing again and again? Look to see how enjoyable your day-to-day activities are, such as mealtimes. Does everyone eat at the counter and then bolt and run? Is the TV set on during mealtimes or do you take time for relaxed conversation with one another? Are most evenings spent together or in separate rooms with individual TV sets? What are the rituals that you are building inside your family?

Questions Parents Ask

Q: We really do try hard to be supportive parents and understand what it means to be fair and reasonable, but Sarah is just plain difficult and has been since birth. We don't have the same thing with her brother and sister, and she just wears us out with her demands and lack of responsibility. Any suggestions?

A: Every child is different, as you've already noticed. Temperament, personality, and the way children personally perceive their world all play into this. Much as we don't want to label a child as "difficult," the truth is that some *are* more demanding, defiant, stubborn, negative, whiny, or impulsive than others. That said, certain responses can make things even more difficult.

Dr. Stanley Turecki,[8] who has spent it a career trying to better understand children who have been termed "difficult," provides parents with some basic facts, i.e., that these children usually *are* normal (that *difficult* does not mean *abnormal*), but admittedly tougher to handle. Because of their innate makeup or temperament, they can be harder to raise. He reminds parents that difficult children are not all the same but admits that they can all make their parents feel angry, inadequate or guilty. He says that sometimes parents of these children become so caught up or irritated that they respond to virtually everything the child does. The more they overreact, the more the child misbehaves, eventually craving the excessive attention her undesirable behavior elicits. He suggests that parents decide what's relative and important and what isn't. Decide what's unacceptable and what you have to take a stand on. In other words, choose your battles.

We have a choice when nothing seems to be working. We can allow our children to continue to create marital strain, family discord, problems with their brothers and sisters, and end up with emotional problems of their own OR we can move them in the direction of becoming positive, enthusiastic, even especially creative individuals. Some of the most charismatic people of the last century, Eleanor Roosevelt, Albert Einstein, Thomas Edison, and Pablo Picasso were notably stubborn and considered odd and difficult to raise by their parents and teachers.

So—what to do? First of all, develop an understanding of what you're dealing with. Turecki's book, *The Difficult Child*,[9] covers a great deal of important information about how to cope effectively with hard-to-raise children. While we have limited space here, we agree with the 6 steps he believes parents need to consider when dealing with negative behavior:

1. Ask yourself, "Can I deal with this now?" Take stock of your own state of mind—for example, how tense or tired are you? If you can't deal calmly with the child's behavior, disengage. Get yourself or your child out of the situation if possible (ex. if your child throws a tantrum in a store, leave). If you're okay, deal with it.

2. Stay in control and be objective about what's going on. Keep your emotions out of it (You're the adult, the boss) and evaluate what your options are for dealing with the situation.

3. Focus completely on the behavior, not what you think the child's motives are (to irritate you, to manipulate you, to get his/her way).

4. Ask, "Can he/she help it?" If it's something that has more to do with temperament than not and you've seen it before, be firm, make eye contact, and proceed to manage the child rather than yelling, strong-arming, or punishing. What needs to happen?

5. Ask, "Is it relevant? Can I let this behavior go and ignore it? Will I lose power or will the situation become worse by doing nothing?" If you decide that it's not temperament but just plain uncooperative, negative behavior that the child CAN manage (has done so in the past), take a stand. It's important to do so.

6. React effectively. Be brief. Use the steps that we described earlier in this chapter. Reflect. Tell the child he/she can either do what you've asked or (name the consequence). Make the consequence equal to the behavior. Don't over-explain or over-talk. Don't moralize, judge, or shame. Offer one warning and one warning only, don't count, and don't negotiate. ALWAYS follow through.

Q: Our kids, 3 and 5, have plenty, but they just don't want to share what they have with each other—ever! I get tired of refereeing and sorting out what they're always fighting about. Is there an answer to this?

A: Well, you can start by not refereeing and sorting out what they're fighting about unless someone is getting hurt or bullied. Try to let them work it out without getting involved. If they come to you to solve the problem, tell them, "I might solve it one way, but the two of you must have some ideas about what's fair here and how to take care of it. I want you to solve your own problems. What are your ideas?" Listen. Make sure each of them listens as well, and make sure each child contributes something reasonable. Don't allow name-calling, yelling, or any physical interactions. Sum up what they've suggested and ask, "What do you think you should do?" If they can't work it out or aren't willing to talk about it, isolate whatever it is that they're fighting over until they can. We're hoping that you have established a rule in your house about privacy and ownership so that if one of the children is violating that rule (ex. taking another person's things without asking), there should be related consequences.

Q: Our son is always bargaining. "If I clean up my room this morning, can we go to the toy store for some Lego blocks?" is an example. He also thinks he should get paid for the chores he's expected to do around the house and gets resentful when we tell him that everyone lives in the house and everyone should help without expecting to get paid. My dad jokes that Alex is just an early "entrepreneur." I think he's very manipulative and lazy on top of it. How do I handle this?

A: Oh, oh. A couple of red flags here! Be careful about negatively labeling your child (lazy…manipulative…). If you believe your child is old enough to begin earning an allowance, try to bring some balance to this situation by having some chores that he *should do* without being paid so that he is contributing to the family's well- being—and then some others that he is paid a reasonable amount for. Discuss this with your child, providing rationale about why you think it's fair to handle it this way. For responsibilities that he is expected to take (homework, feeding the dog, making his bed), don't negotiate. If he chooses not to follow through on those, don't ignore the lapse. Attach a logical or related consequence (ex. Eliminating the extra chores he's getting paid for or no TV until everything is completed). For the other, which you've agreed to pay him for, make sure he understands that he should let you know if he's unable to take care of it so that you can make other arrangements.

Q: We have a really mouthy kid, much as I hate to admit it. He loves to shock everyone and is liable to come out with something in front of people at the worst times, and it just embarrasses us. He uses language that we don't, argues just for the sake of arguing, and is pretty disrespectful. He's been tough to deal with, and we haven't had much luck in controlling this.

A: This is where family identity comes into play in a big way. As calmly as you can, talk with your son about the fact that you want to be proud of him as he grows up and that there are certain behavior standards that are important in your family. Explain that when he's in front of others, he really is an ambassador who lets others know what your family's values are, that it makes others uncomfortable when he argues or is disrespectful, and that you have to depend on him to reasonably filter his thoughts, language, and behavior so that others see him (and his family) in the best possible light. Use a firm, authoritative tone of voice and good eye contact when talking with him about this so that he realizes the seriousness of what you're saying. Let him know exactly what you believe is inappropriate and won't be tolerated. Talk with your spouse about what you both will do if your son does not respect your wishes about this. If he chooses not to comply, follow through on corrective consequences that were discussed earlier with him.

Q: How do you feel about spanking? I'm not talking about abuse, just 5 or 6 slaps on my daughter's behind when she's been sassy or misbehaved. I want her to know I mean business, and it seems this is the only way to get her to listen to me.

A: People have strong opinions about spanking or not spanking, although most lean today in the direction of choosing some other method of discipline. I favor that for a number of reasons. One is personal. I wouldn't want anyone hitting or slapping me—not for any reason. Let's be honest. That's really what spanking is. I admit that it does get children to do what you're asking, but not out of respect, wanting to cooperate, or having learned a better way to behave. Physical punishment comes at an emotional price. Kids feel ashamed, embarrassed, angry, fearful, and resentful. It doesn't teach them a new behavior skill, only what NOT to do when you're looking. It also teaches them how to be aggressive toward others who are weaker than they are. It only continues to work when children are small and usually leaves spanking parents at a loss for how to discipline children when they're too big to hit anymore. Your alternative to spanking is to tell her clearly what to do in a firm, calm, and authoritative voice. If she doesn't comply in a reasonable time, give a warning ("You can either…or…"). Remember that the consequence should be related to the behavior whenever possible, but if you need to use an unrelated one, do so. Follow through so that she knows she'd better do what you ask and not test you out.

Red Flags That Signal Parenting Problems

1. Children are frequently out of control, uncooperative, irresponsible, or disrespectful.

2. Parents disagree on how to discipline the children or undermine one another.

3. Children have learned to manipulate one or both parents.

4. One or more family members is unhappy or depressed.

5. The family has a chaotic lifestyle, and parents spend little time with their children.

6. There is teasing, taunting, bullying, psychological, or physical abuse in the family.

7. The family is isolated from the extended family and/or friends.

8. There are no rules or standards in the family for behavior—or rules are applied in an inconsistent and arbitrary manner.

9. The family is experiencing severe financial difficulty so that children's needs are not cared for.

10. The dominant parenting style is uninvolved, permissive, or authoritarian.

What's in Your Parenting Toolkit?

1. Be authoritative. Be firm and reason with children when possible but maintain control in the situation and apply constructive consequences and follow-through processes.

2. Use personal messages. Reflect the child's behavior. Describe your own emotions and a reason why you want the child to change his/her behavior. Point out a more acceptable behavior you DO want to see.

3. Use natural or logical consequences when necessary to redirect behavior. Use unrelated consequences only when nothing else is working.

4. Be consistent. Don't ignore behavior one time and jump on it the next.

5. When children are out of line, give a clear warning and state a clear consequence. NEVER, NEVER, NEVER warn children twice or count (1...2...3...) after telling them what to do. Be quiet and give them a reasonable time to comply; if they don't, always follow through.

6. Have few rules but do not ignore behavior that you don't want to see again. Do not allow bullying, abuse, shaming, name calling, or disrespect.

7. Even if you can, do not give children everything they want. Provide for needs and support them in their own efforts to get things they want.

8. Spend individual time with each child to build rapport and time together and as a family to build memories and a family identity together.

9. If there is continuing stress, a lack of healthy communication, or hostile behavior in the family, get competent, professional help to make a change.

10. When the discipline you're using doesn't seem to be working, review the steps in this chapter for dealing with children's negative behaviors. Are there steps you're missing or implementing poorly?

Conclusion

In this chapter, we've outlined 6 parenting principals that will serve as a foundation for meeting the challenges that children naturally present, for making the hard decisions that are sometimes tough to face up to, and for working as a team to provide the security and effective guidance to produce healthy children and a healthy family context. In the days ahead, be especially vigilant about deterrents to authoritative parenting. These can include a lack of consistency in applying needed corrective consequences, power struggles between family members, your own lack of motivation to try new strategies for more effective parenting, or an overscheduled lifestyle. Also, in the chapters that follow, you'll see references back to these six principles as they apply to specific areas of and issues surrounding your child's development. Keep the future in mind as well as being mindful of what's going on currently. Make the necessary commitment to interact in ways that will produce the favorable results you want, both in the short term and in the long run.

CHAPTER 2

The Emotionally Healthy and Resilient Child

Many years ago, I ran into the work of Urie Bronfenbrenner, a well-known psychologist at Cornell University. He said something that left a profound mark on me: "Every child needs at least one adult who is irrationally crazy about him or her."[10] I thought a lot about that "one adult" he was talking about. It didn't necessarily have to be a parent or grandparent and, of course, it would take more than one person eventually to guide a child toward adolescence and adulthood. However, if that one affectionate adult is initially missing, and a child has no one who "is crazy" about him or her, no one who cares deeply in the very early years, that child may somehow become flawed as a human being. That adult who is so critically important in a child's life doesn't always have to be perfect and won't be. Someone just needs to be there—and care.

In this chapter, we're going to look at the beginnings of being human, the building of the emotional self and the role of temperament in that process. We'll also consider how resilience and stress hardiness emerge in an emotionally healthy child.

How Emotions Develop

Each day, a child experiences a variety of emotions that are triggered by external events. In milliseconds, those occurrences send signals to the brain that, in turn, create physical, expressive, and cognitive responses that all work together to create an emotional reaction in any particular situation.[11] For example, Randi's dad gives her a hug before she leaves for school. Later, a classmate says something hurtful. Another one notices and says, "Never mind. She's so mean. Let's eat lunch together today, okay?" The school serves pizza for lunch, a favorite—and then, the teacher chooses Randi to read something she's written. One classmate snickers, but three kids clap when she finishes. Playing jump rope after school is frustrating, followed by finally getting twelve jumps in a row before missing. The day goes like that for Randi—some positive emotional experiences and some negative, but a pretty good balance and leaning on the side of positive ones. Another child's day may be very different and perhaps not nearly as upbeat.

Children don't come equipped with all those emotions at birth and, depending on their day-to-day experiences and interactions with others in their world, some emotions became stronger or weaker than others, just as some of our neural pathways become stronger or grow weaker depending on our experiences.

As parents, we're thrilled to see that first primary emotion of joy expressed in a child's smile at about 6 weeks (gas will do that as well!). Then, as intellectual development continues, other emotions begin to surface. Anger appears between 4-6 months, sadness about 5-7 months, and fear between 5-12 months. Joy, anger, sadness, and fear: those are the big four and, from there, those primary emotions branch out into corresponding emotional clusters. For example, fear will manifest itself in other emotions, such as wariness between 5-7 months, shyness between 8-10 months, stranger distress and separation anxiety by the end of the first year and then in a variety of other emotions such as shame, guilt, empathy, worry, dread, concern, panic, anxiety, and suspicion as a child grows older and experiences more of life. The same thing is true of the other primary emotions of joy, anger, and sadness.[12]

Between birth and about 1 year of age, depending on how well a child's needs are being met, she learns to trust or mistrust others, according to psychologist Erik Erikson.[13] Autonomy (the child's striving for independence) vs. shame and doubt ("I can do this!" vs "I'm not very good at this.") follow in years 1-3. Erikson believed that initiative (learning resourceful ways of acting on ideas) vs. guilt (shame and self-reproach) are the emotional tasks the child works through from 3-6 years. These are followed by industry (feeling productive and successful) vs. inferiority from 6-12 years. Still more emotional stages of development and tasks to accomplish continue lifelong as we interact initially with our parents, family members, and early caregivers and then later on with peers, teachers, business associates, and many others. How well we do later on in life depends on how well the earlier stages go, whether the outcomes are mostly positive or mostly negative, and subsequent experiences that may impact significantly on a person.

There are particular lessons that children must learn in early childhood, and they need an adult's help in doing so. Very young children don't necessarily understand that everyone else has emotions and that people give off social cues to let others know how they're feeling. Some children never become skilled at recognizing those social cues. Early on, they fail to learn that emotions are prompted by different situations and that there are different ways to express emotions—both positive and negative. We support that growth in our children when we name emotions they're seeing or feeling: "Look at Raymond's face. He's furious because you pushed him." "You're sad that the dog chewed your teddy bear's leg." "You were delighted at gymnastics today when you could finally do that back flip. I was glad for you."

There are multiple other ways we can teach them about emotions. We can sing songs with them about emotions, read picture books that tell stories about emotions, and share our own emotions with them, using a varied vocabulary "This made me so happy (pleased, glad, delighted, grateful)," "I was sad (disappointed, upset, discouraged, sorry, ashamed, worried) when…," "I felt afraid (concerned, uncomfortable, worried, scared) when…" [14] Without blaming, judging, or moralizing, we can talk with them after events that spark particularly intense emotional reactions from them.

Affective reflections are a powerful way to let children know we're paying attention to them and respect how they're feeling. They can be part of those two-part or three-part personal messages that we talked about in Chapter 1. Following are some examples:

> **Situation:** Your three-year-old is balking when asked to clean up.
> **Your affective reflection:** "You wish you didn't have to clean up."

> **Situation:** It's time to leave the playground, and your five-year-old doesn't want to.
> **Your affective reflection:** "You're unhappy about having to leave right now."

> **Situation:** Your 10-year-old is playing a video game, and his three-year-old sister keeps telling him she wants to play. You can see that he's growing irritated with her, and you are ready to step in if she doesn't listen and keeps pestering him.
> **Your affective reflection to your son:** "You're really annoyed with her."

Situation: Your 12-year-old daughter gets off the phone and jumps up and down about being invited to a classmate's birthday party.

Your affective reflection to her: "You're ecstatic that Tricia invited you. I'm happy for you."

Affective reflections teach children to differentiate emotions they may be feeling, to learn that emotions are normal in themselves and others, and to provide the vocabulary of emotions. When we remind them in certain circumstances to "use their words," it helps to teach them ahead of time words or statements they can use to diffuse a situation or just let others know how they're feeling about something.

Before you say anything in a tense situation, however, be careful to watch your children's facial expression, voice tone, and posture, just so you don't misinterpret how they might *really* be feeling. Sometimes, what they say is not how they're feeling inside, and this can be especially true of older children who might try to hide their true feelings with words that don't match their external demeanor.[15] We can miss the mark entirely and, in doing so, actually increase their disappointment, anger, or other true feelings. Also, we can make the situation worse if we suggest in any way that what they're saying is not how they're really feeling. When we're unsure, it may be better to make a simple, nonjudgmental assessment: "You look upset," and then stay quiet if they don't want to talk about it right then.

With guidance, they also learn that other people may not feel exactly the same way they do and that they can do something to affect how they feel and how others feel. This has to do with their development of empathy and ability to feel what others are feeling, a critical human emotion. We can see it as early as 18 months in a child trying to comfort someone who is upset or hurt and more strongly around the age of 5 or 6 as intellectual reasoning develops. Not ever seeing it is highly problematic.

Empathy goes beyond sympathy, and it's important to recognize that they are not the same thing. Sympathy has to do with feeling bad for a person who is uncomfortable or in pain. Empathy allows human beings to actually share an emotional experience with the person, to be able to feel what the person is feeling and take the person's perspective, and then be motivated to help in some way.[16] With young children, that may include their patting or hugging the person, bringing them something to ease the situation such as a tissue or helping them get what they need. It may involve a child helping a peer who is being bullied or feeling sorry that they have hurt another child and trying to make restitution in some way—an attempt to make it all right again.

Remember that children who have uninvolved, authoritarian, or permissive parents may not learn to regulate negative emotions, develop feelings for others, or experience guilt for inappropriate or hurtful actions toward others. That's because they've had poor models or no model at all. The results of what has been termed "emotional illiteracy" are costly in society.[17] We see abusive teenagers or adults with worrisome levels of anger and depression and who are likely to have higher rates of addiction, crime, and violence. They are less likely to care about others and, worse yet, they may lack the moral conscience that kicks in to make us feel uneasy when we have not been fair-minded, kind, or honest with others.[18]

Emotional IQ and Executive Function (EF)

An ability to identify and manage their emotions will be the key to your child's future success in getting along well with others—and life, in general. I can't stress that more strongly. Without it, they will be unable to communicate well with others, understand when they are feeling safe or not safe, or make solid connections between what they're thinking and feeling. Children with poorly developed emotional IQ have trouble resolving conflicts with others in a nonviolent way. They may lack empathy for others and recover poorly from setbacks they experience. Five specific skills they need for developing *emotional intelligence*[19, 20, 21] (literally, to become emotionally smart) include the following:

1. **Self-awareness**—Knowing what they know and don't know about themselves; being mindful of their own thoughts, feelings and strengths and how they impact their behavior

2. **Social awareness**—Having empathy and respect for others and taking into consideration the thoughts, feelings, and perspectives of others

3. **Self-management**—Controlling their emotions and impulses in order to accomplish what they need to; staying organized and prioritizing tasks; setting goals and resolving hurdles that get in the way; managing time

4. **Responsible decision making**—Taking in information and making sense of it; being able to create, carry out, and assess effective solutions to problems and to evaluate the effects of their decisions on themselves and others; seeking help when they're stuck and need it.

5. **Relationship skills**—Resolving differences in opinions with others while still maintaining positive connections with them; resisting negative peer pressure.[22]

You can see why authoritative parenting supports the development of emotional IQ and how other parenting styles actually inhibit it. When parents encourage children to think about and talk about their behavior and feelings, as well as their perceptions of what others may be thinking or feeling, self-awareness and social awareness are promoted. When constructive consequences are employed, rather than punishment, and children are actively guided in making good decisions, greater self-regulation is the outcome. All of this results in a child's ability to get along well with others and to lead a relatively satisfying and successful life.

Also operating to produce self-regulation and emotional intelligence in children is *executive function* or EF. It involves cognitive processes that develop in the preschool years and beyond, requiring such abilities as self-awareness, non-verbal and verbal working memory, self-motivation, and emotional self-regulation. Also included are problem solving, making transitions from one thing to another, organizational and inhibition abilities. Not everyone looks at executive function in exactly the same way but, obviously, when there are deficits in these skills, children will have problems with impulse control and curbing emotional outbursts. There will likely be an incapacity to focus and failure to take responsibility, manage time, and adapt in situations when needed. These are kids who may score within normal ranges on an I. Q. test but "just don't get it." They have trouble with storage and retrieval (particularly required for success in spelling and math), routine transitions, and staying on task. Exasperated parents and teachers find them unable to connect consequences to the behaviors that caused them, and it certainly does little good to say, "Why didn't you think about it before you did that?" because that's exactly the problem. They can't.

Physician Ira J. Chasnoff has warned parents that because executive functioning involves a wide spectrum of brain functioning, it is highly vulnerable to prenatal exposure to tobacco, alcohol, and illicit drugs and to avoid these at all costs during pregnancy.[23] Also, there can be a genetic predisposition involved and, without specialized and competent support, a child's lack of executive function can lead to parents feeling guilty and overwhelmed, the child seeing himself as a failure, and other unacceptable and detrimental outcomes. More about this and ways in which parents can support executive function will be discussed in Chapter 4.

Temperament and Personality

If you have more than one child, you already know that there can be dramatic differences between them in terms of their temperament and personality, and you probably began to notice this as early as 2-3 months. Influenced by more than 700 genes,[24] temperament is a child's strong disposition to react in certain ways to what's going on in their world. Personality is different. It is definitely influenced by temperament but is ultimately modified in certain ways by people and events in children's lives as they grow older. Each person develops a distinct character that is an outcome of native temperament and interaction with his/her environment.

Although there are differing descriptions of the individual characteristics that make up temperament,[25] with most of the studies conducted in the 80s, the following nine are often cited in long-standing and reliable studies about this inborn aspect in children:

1. **Activity level**—High motor activity vs passive inactivity

2. **Rhythmicity**—Strong internal timeclock and predictability relative to eating, sleeping, and elimination patterns vs scattered regularity

3. **Approach and Withdrawal**—Initial responses to new objects, people, experiences

4. **Adaptability**—Positive or negative response to change over time

5. **Intensity of Reaction**—Energy level in response to stimuli

6. **Responsiveness Threshold**—High or low sensitivity to a variety of stimuli (ex. noise, touch, smell, temperature, light, color, etc.)

7. **Mood**—Positive vs negative state

8. **Attention Span and Resistance**—Willingness to spend time on a pursuit

9. **Distractibility**—Vulnerability to interference when on task

Taken together, these 9 different attributes cluster into three basic types of temperament: easy, difficult, and slow-to-warm up. And, because temperament is biological, natural, and genetic, it's not always simple to modify or change it. *Easy* children (about 40% of all children studied) are moderately low in intensity, adaptable, approachable, predictable with body functions, and positive in mood. Even as infants, they're generally happy, busy, and friendly—and they tend to stay that way through childhood and beyond. Change is usually not a problem with them, and in fact, they rather enjoy it. They're easier to feed, easier to toilet train, and fall into bedtime routines fairly well. If you only have one child, and that child has an easy temperament and personality, you might give yourself more credit for your parenting skills than you ought to!

Conversely, *difficult* children (about 10%) tend to keep us humble. They are more often negative in mood, adapt slowly to change, are less predictable with respect to biological functions, and frequently exhibit intense reactions. They can easily produce guilt in us, a sense of helplessness, and worry about the future. Parents who are doing their best may be embarrassed by others' reactions to the child's lack of control, tantrums, and challenging behaviors.

Slow-to-warm-up children take longer to adapt in unfamiliar situations, are more passive, and less intensive. They make up about 15 percent of children studied, while another 35 percent, a sizeable group, don't seem to fit neatly into any of these three categories. Slow-to-warm up kids can present challenges when parents are impatient or not very understanding about their inability to adapt easily to change or to new situations and people. They may become annoyed or even embarrassed when their child is shy, hangs back while other children charge into play situations, or doesn't seem to appreciate surprises and opportunities for new activities. While someone else's child might be excited about the beginning of the school year, a slow-to-warm up child might be dreading it.

If your child can be classified as *easy*, congratulations. However, if she's in that group that makes up those determined as more *difficult*, then you'll need to be careful about the ways in which you react to that negativity, particularly if your own temperament leans in that direction. Ways in which you choose to deal with a difficult or slow-to-warm up child may have long-lasting effects on a child's emerging personality. The wrong way to go would be to ignore difficult behavior, shame or compare children to others, label a child with derogatory words, or inflict verbal or physical punishment. Remember that the child is not intentionally being stubborn or difficult and isn't out there trying to make your life miserable. However, if power struggles have been going on for a while and have become an established interpersonal problem between the two of you, you'll want to consider getting the help of a good family therapist—for both your sake and the child's.

There are better ways to respond that will keep the child's self-esteem intact and contribute to a more positive and cooperative personality in the long run. Most important is respecting the child, keeping in mind that individual differences can be the result of heredity and the environment, not because you're incompetent as a parent or because the child is intentionally being difficult or stubborn.

When there's a tough situation, take a look at the circumstances to see if you can work out a plan with the child to help her cope more constructively. Ask yourself if your own temperamental style and personality are getting in the way. Is there something about your behavior—or your partner's behavior—that could be changed in order to work more effectively with the child?[26]

Consider what these parents were saying in a parent education meeting at Brentwood Middle School:

> **Lila:** I remember that when my son Mike was small and we got together with his older, well behaved cousins, I wanted to be proud of him and have him toe the line every bit as well as the older boys. Later, when I thought more about it, I was expecting way too much of him, given the age and personality differences. It had a lot to do with my pride as a mother, I think. Actually, it was something my son said to me: "Mom, you always think that they're perfect, and I'm not, don't you?" It was true and while I still needed to set reasonable and effective limits, I realized that I needed to be more patient. It was also a chance in a less threatening atmosphere to talk with him about correcting the behavior that had upset me.

> **Don:** I had no doubt that I was going to have another perfect kid. When Nicole came along, we treated her the same way we did with her older sister Karen but, boy, Nicole could throw a tantrum in ways that Karen never thought

about doing. When Nicole didn't get her way, she would get that look on her face and we would know an explosion was coming. It didn't matter where we were or who was around. She was doing the same thing at school. The two girls could not have been any different and, to tell the truth, we weren't handling it very well. A lot of what we were trying was just making things worse.

Ellie: Something that really was embarrassing was when we would have company over. Vince was different than our other kids about that. The girls loved it, but he was always shy and a little nervous in front of our adult friends—and when that happened and without realizing it, he had a habit of masturbating. So, there we all were in the kitchen talking when he walked in and as soon as someone said, "How's it going, Vince?" his hand shot straight to his genitals. I had talked with him about it after it had happened the second time. I didn't want to make a big deal about it but just mentioned that it probably made other people feel uncomfortable. He understood. Anyway, we came up with a plan—a code between just the two of us and something I would say that would alert him about it. So, the next time it occurred and without missing a beat, I simply said, "Did you remember to feed the dog today?" That was the "secret" cue. He got the message, and without having to be embarrassed, he corrected the situation and answered "Yep." And we actually got a smile out of him!

Lindsay: Going to church with the kids was getting to be a nightmare. Rob was okay and probably could sit for hours with his own thoughts and be fine, but Mitch was only all right for about 15 minutes or so. Then, no matter how many times we talked with him about it or warned him, he would start getting fidgety and look for ways to annoy Rob. He just couldn't sit still that long and just listen to what the minister was saying. We made two changes. First of all, my wife or I sat between the boys, creating a little distance between them, and Mitch brought along a coloring book and markers. We were a little embarrassed when people sitting nearby seemed to disapprove, but it solved the problem. We know Mitch will get rid of the coloring book deal as he gets older. Maybe when he's thirty!

Karen Stephens, past director of Illinois State University's Child Care Center has had plenty of experience with young children making sense of their world. When interviewed about children with difficult temperaments, she offered a number of excellent suggestions, including the following:

Avoid name-calling and labeling kids as "hyper," "problem child" or "trouble-maker." Labels chip away at self-esteem.

Use reflection to help children recognize options. "It looks like that sweater feels too scratchy. Can you find something in your closet that feels better?"

If your child is overwhelmed by too many choices, limit the number. "Here are two videos you can watch. Which one do you choose?"

Make sure kids get hands-on active play daily; it helps them use energy constructively. A children's discovery museum engages these kids more than going to a sit-down children's concert. Avoid over-scheduling children but consider a lesson that's a good outlet for energy, such as swimming, gymnastics, or dance lessons.

Provide more structure if a child regularly becomes overwhelmed and loses control. Maintain predictable wake-up and bedtimes, regular snack and mealtimes, and have a plan for what will happen each day. On errands, provide structure by giving the child a job to do, such as to look for a specific type of cereal as you shop.

Respect children's preferences in terms of food taste, scent, and texture. It's counter-productive to force a child to eat an egg salad sandwich if it comes up in two seconds. Model flexibility by serving food in a way your child can better tolerate.

Coach children towards self-control. Every child can be impulsive, but especially spirited children. Help them master language to express feelings. Remind them to find non-aggressive ways to achieve goals.

Help children regain control during or after tantrums. "You're yelling too loud. When you speak more quietly, I'll listen." "Here's a tissue for your tears. Find another way to show me what you want." "You're so frustrated that you're throwing a fit. Breathe slower and more deeply; it can help you calm down."

Choose your battles wisely. Avoid power struggles. When disciplining, use clear direction and enforce age-appropriate limits with reasonable, related, and respectful consequences. Avoid over-reacting, raising your voice, or issuing false threats and ultimatums. Deal with behavior problems calmly and matter-of-factly. This will help your child gain control and develop trust in your support and guidance.[27]

A final word about temperament and personality is that you will want to consider what is called "goodness of fit" with your child. How much are you alike or different in terms of your own temperaments and personalities? For example, if you would describe yourself as fairly quiet and laid back and you are gifted with a very active and expressive child, there could be goodness of fit if you can appreciate that child's energy and liveliness. However, if you view his get-up-and-go and vitality as something that drives you crazy and something you often need relief from, that's not a good fit. That doesn't mean it can't get better.

Because you're the adult, a young child must rely on you to take the steps necessary to shape a "goodness of fit" relationship, one that will be satisfying for a lifetime between the two of you. If it's a good one already, you'll know it because you'll both look forward to spending time together. If not, examine how well your reactions, expectations, and responses to your child's behavioral style make life difficult for the two of you. Think about whether there are changes needed to create a more compatible match or accommodate differences in a more effective and respectful way. That sometimes requires seeking constructive advice and help when you've exhausted your own resources. Remember that you play a critical role in having your child feel accepted and valued and that you are someone who has significant influence over your child's developing personality. You want it to go in the right direction.

Resilience and Stress Hardiness

This year, as I write this book, we've all been tested as a human race more than at any other time in which we've lived. The Covid-19 virus has killed millions world-wide, all but destroyed our U. S. economy, shut down the things we like to do for recreation and fun, interrupted education globally, and shut us away from one another socially. Political differences have become challenging and dangerous. If there has ever been a time when our resilience is being tested, it is now.

According to Kenneth Ginsburg, author of *Building Resilience in Children and Teens: Giving Kids Roots and Wings*, "Resilience is the capacity to rise above difficult circumstances, the trait that allows us to exist in this less-than-perfect world while moving forward with optimism and confidence even in the midst of adversity."[28] That's exactly what we want for our children. It's an insurance policy that provides a righting factor to recover from stressful events they are sure to encounter.

While resilient children are not all alike or resilient in every circumstance, they do share some of the same characteristics we see in socially competent children. They can best be described as "emotionally, physically, cognitively, and socially put together."[29] They don't buckle easily in times of significant adversity. Because they feel valued (not always by their parents but by some adult), have purpose, enjoy being helpful to others, and consistently demonstrate self-control and responsibility, they're generally happy, optimistic, and well behaved. Both adults and peers like being around them. What is crucial for us to consider is how certain kids get this way—or don't.

Resilience develops from a combination of temperament attributes and growing up in fundamentally strong physical and cultural systems, i.e., everything that surrounds a child—family, peer groups, schools, and social and political communities. When these *adaptive systems* function well to buffer stress and adversity, resilience results. When they don't, children embedded within them can become vulnerable and less able to stay on track developmentally. It's believed that the child's temperament and personality will also have an effect on how a child copes with stress and adversity.

How much do you know about how your children handle stress? What's going on in their individual world? Think about those adaptive systems surrounding each of them. How are they doing at home in terms of taking responsibility and interacting with other family members? Are they connected with extended family members on both sides of the family, such as grandparents? How often are they in touch with them?

Are they attending a good school? How would you rate it? Are teachers supportive? Do each of your children have a good friend his or her own age? What kind of kids are they making friends with and do they share your values? Do you know the parents of their friends? What kinds of activities are they choosing to be involved with and how active are they? How much leisure time does each of them spend on technology?

The reason I'm asking these questions is because we need to check in every now and then with what's going on in each of our children's life. We get busy just taking care of day-to-day responsibilities, and we have all kinds of things that can legitimately divert our attention from parenting. Also, the older our children get, the less we may be tuned in. For their own good, we want them to become less dependent on us, making their own decisions and solving their own problems. The last thing in the world we want is to be one of those helicopter parents we've all heard about, constantly overindulging, overprotecting, and overseeing every aspect of our children's lives.

Every child will encounter stress. That's just a fact of life. There will be normal ones, such as not getting invited to a birthday party or losing at a game. Most kids can handle that. When a risk factor is added, such as separation and divorce of parents (see Chapter 5), kids can usually cope pretty well if certain assets and protective factors are present. Ann Masten, a faculty member at University of Minnesota, believes that resilience isn't the result of anything special, but comes from most children growing up in well-operating fundamental adaptive systems.[30] These include the following:

Child Characteristics

- An adaptive temperament
- Good cognitive abilities and problem-solving skills
- Effective emotional and behavioral regulations strategies
- Self-confidence, high self-esteem, self-efficacy
- A positive outlook on life
- Faith and a sense of meaning in life
- Characteristics valued by society and self (talents, sense of humor, attractiveness to others)

Family Characteristics

- Stable and supportive home environment
  - Low level of parental discord
  - Close relationship to responsive caregiver
  - Authoritative parenting style
  - Positive sibling relationships
  - Supportive connections with extended family members
- Parents involved in children's education
- Socioeconomic advantages
- Postsecondary education of parent
- Faith and religious affiliations

Community Characteristics

- High neighborhood quality (ex. low violence, affordable housing, clean air and water)
- Effective schools (ex. well-trained and well-compensated teachers, after-school programs)
- Employment opportunities for parents and teens
- Good public health care
- Access to emergency services (police, fire, medical)
- Connections to caring adult mentors and prosocial peers

Cultural or Societal Characteristics

- Protective child policies (child labor, child health, and child welfare)
- Value and resources directed at education
- Prevention of and protection from oppression or political violence
- Low acceptance of physical violence[31]

When a child has these kinds of adaptive systems surrounding her, she has the kind of support needed to keep development and resilience on track. However, to the extent that there are multiple risk factors such as mental health problems (especially with a mother), parental abuse, peer factors such as substance abuse, or poverty, resilience and the ability to stay on track developmentally will be challenged without increased protective factors and surveillance. Then, with adversity, such as disease, loss of a parent, home, or adequate health care and nutrition, we can expect there will be failure of a child to cope, predictable vulnerability, and loss of resilience without intervention.

There are children who become what we call "stress-hardy." That doesn't mean that they're invulnerable to stress or able to avoid it. None of us can do that. *Stress hardiness* is an individual personality quality that helps to explain why some kids are more resilient and able to bounce back during or after multiple risks or adversity. It might be said that they are their own most important protective factor. They are less likely to lose control in the face of stressful events, perceive stressful events as less threatening than others might, and tend to see a stressful event as a learning experience. They are also more likely to be optimistic and to consistently anticipate an "okay" outcome when experiencing stressful events or adversity.

Optimism can be taught, and it's especially important to teach it to children who tend toward negativity. We need to let children know that they do have control over optimism versus pessimism. Again, we can point out those qualities in people they know who don't experience any more difficulties in life than anyone else but who seem to stay focused on the difficulty instead of on possibilities for relief, redirection, and getting on with life. Talk with your children about people they know that are upbeat and more enjoyable to be around, who have a sense of humor, and a positive outlook on life. Children's literature and films are a great resource. Help them discover books, videos, and movies where the characters experience problems and don't give up, with a favorable result as the outcome. If you hear negative self-talk ("I'm no good at this!" "Nobody really likes me at school." "I'll never finish this homework assignment on time." "I suck at sports."), bring the negativity to their attention and encourage them to develop a more positive, energy-producing mindset instead of one that drags them down. Model the practice of keeping a journal in which you write at least one good thing that happened that day—or maybe three.

Optimism is a choice. It's a frame of mind, a way of thinking about challenges and viewing them with the belief that there can usually be a way to change a situation into a more positive direction. When we discourage negative references in themselves or with respect to others, we increase a child's self-determination and self-efficacy by teaching them positive self-talk: ("I can handle this." "I can figure this out if I stay calm." "I've made some progress here. It's making a difference."). Optimism is life with persistent hopefulness.

Conversely, children who develop poor psychological health and feelings of helplessness[32] develop patterns of expecting poor outcomes. They feel helpless and powerless to change situations that bother them, anything about themselves, or ways to interact in a more positive way with others. What these children lack is what resilient children have developed: behavior that demonstrates they are motivated, creative, flexible, adaptable, and open to change. They take an active approach toward problem solving, are self-starters, and like people. As a result, people almost always like them back.[33]

Questions Parents Ask

Q: My husband is really a good father. Don't get me wrong, but he makes fun of my son when he cries about something and tells him, "Don't be a crybaby. Grow up." He's six now, and I can see him starting to hide or deny his feelings when he's hurt about something. When I approach my husband about this, we just get into an argument. He says he doesn't want his son growing up to be weak and to stay out of it.

A: To have deep feelings is to be human, and it's never okay to tell a child—boy or girl—not to cry. Research tells us that male babies and very young boys are just as emotional as little girls—until we teach them not to be. We do that very effectively when we tell them to choke back what they're feeling and just stuff it down. "It's shameful for boys to cry, so stop it!" Unfortunately, emotions have a way of coming out, one way or another. Boys (and then men) in our society do find other ways to deal with their emotions. They become stoic and uncommunicative, shut themselves away emotionally from others, become angry and violent, or cold and unreactive. All that, because it's unmanly to find catharsis through tears. If you feel your son is crying more than normal, look at the bigger picture when this happens. Is he doing it to get attention or simply to get something he wants? Is it part of who he is, part of a more sensitive personality? Does it happen in certain situations more than in others, such as when he's experiencing anxiety or afraid about something? Is it when he's simply out of patience, hungry, tired, or worn out? If so, can you ward any of that off? Usually, as children grow older, they naturally develop ways to handle intense emotions without crying so often. In a supportive environment, they learn that they can tell someone how they're feeling instead of crying. Sometimes, an affective reflection from a caring parent or a hug does it. Older children find private places to let it go, and some find that writing their feelings down in a journal or talking with a best friend can help. This is too important for you to "stay out of it." See if your husband is open to discussing this with a professional skilled in this issue, if only to have him learn more about the consequences of shutting down your son's emotions. Look for ways to help your son find additional outlets for expressing his feelings when he's sad, afraid, or disappointed.

Q: When is it too late to develop an optimistic personality? When I think about it, I'm really not a very positive person, and I'm afraid some of that has rubbed off on my 10-year-old daughter. I hear a lot of that negative self-talk coming out of her.

A: Optimistically? It's never too late. Marvin Seligman[34] has written about his road to becoming an optimistic person when he was told by his young daughter that he was a grouch. Admittedly, if we have a difficult temperament, and a fair amount of people do, it's almost natural to become somewhat pessimistic. We can turn this around. The remedy is catching ourselves being negative, stopping it, admitting it, and actively seeking how to reframe the event, or leave the event behind us. We also need to be more careful about viewing or labeling other people in an unconstructive way. To make positive changes in our children, model that behavior and admit in front of them what you're doing, that you're trying to become more optimistic and have a more constructive outlook on life. You'll soon see them doing the same thing. For very young children, look for a little book called "*The Little Brute Family*" by Russell and Lillian Hoban.

Q: We never had any problems with our two-year old until his little brother was born. Michael was really jealous, right from the start. It wasn't long after we had brought John home from the hospital that I heard him crying. When I went to check on him, I found a scratch across his eyelid. Michael was standing nearby the crib, looking very guilty. I felt awful because that was the first time that I really felt angry toward Michael, as well as protective about the new baby. I'm really afraid to leave them alone with each other. Should I be?

A: Dr. Barton Schmitt,[35] in discussing aggressive sibling rivalry in children under three years of age, recommends not leaving the older child alone with the baby for at least the first 12 months. Right now, Michael probably feels like he's been replaced, and his emotions may include being angry, upset, sad, and perhaps wanting to be a baby again himself. Not wanting to share you with what he sees as an "intruder" is completely normal for a two-year-old, and it would be unlikely behavior in a much older child. It's important not to scold, try to "fix" the negative emotions, shame him, or use any kind of physical punishment, such as slapping his hands or spanking. That would only make him more resentful and liable to be aggressive again with the baby if he gets the chance. Start with an affective reflection, "You're mad at the baby. I'm upset that you hurt him. We never hurt babies—*ever*. When you feel mad at the baby, come to me for a hug. Remember, hurting is not allowed." You can also offer other things for Michael to do instead of hurting. He can roar and act like a lion, jump up and down, or draw a picture of a mad face. Find time when he goes to bed or the baby is sleeping to snuggle with him or spend one-on-one time together with an activity he enjoys. If he says he doesn't like the baby and wants you to get rid of him, be understanding and accept what he's telling you. Say, "Being a big brother can be hard. I love you, and I want you to feel better." There are a number of children's books to help a young child understand what it is to be an older sibling and to support their acceptance: Simeon's *The Super Incredible Big Brother (or Sister)*; Joanna Cole's *I'm A Big Brother*; Caroline Church's *I Am A Big Brother*; Lucy Topper's *You're* *the Biggest*; and Ashley Moulton's *How to be a Big Brother*; and many others. You can have on hand some little gifts (from the baby, of course) to share with him when grandparents and friends come with all those gifts just for the baby. Take that time to let them oooh and aaaah over the baby and spend a little special time with Michael.

Q: We've recently adopted a little girl who was taken away from her family because of abuse when she was three. She's nine now and has been through a series of foster homes. She's a tough little cookie to deal with. We're committed to not failing her and know how important that is, but we worry that we're not going to be able to fix all the damage. Can kids recover from this kind of harm?

A: You're worried that you might not be able to help her enough. It's amazing how resilient children can be; however, that will depend on her temperament and personality, the amount and kind of trauma to which she's been exposed, and her ability to rise above it. Kenneth Ginsburg[36] has studied resilience in human beings for years and notes that he's never yet met a human being with the capacity to bounce back from every difficult circumstance; yet, he adds that he remains humbled on an almost daily basis by those who have maintained their spirit and optimism in the face of serious adversity. I'm hopeful that will be the case with your daughter. That doesn't mean that she isn't going to wear you out at times, but you've already discovered that and remain committed to her well-being. Remember when we talked about Erik Erikson's belief that human beings had certain tasks they had to work through at certain ages? I think you can assume that she may have some issues with trust, and it may take some time to establish a trusting relationship with her. That will be the most important thing. She has to learn to develop trust in herself and in you and to begin seeing her world as a place where she is safe and where her needs will be met. It's difficult to know where there may be some other concerns or where they may pop up in the future. The best way forward is to be there for her when she will need additional support, to give her plenty of positive attention, avoid power struggles, and to calmly apply corrective consequences when necessary. The other thing is to make sure you take care of yourself in the process so that you can remain healthy and be the constant she will need for a brighter future.

Q: Why do I feel "phony" when I'm using affective reflections? Maybe it's just not "me."

A: You're not keen on using affective reflections. You feel insincere.

Q: Yeah, I do. Why not just talk to your kids?

A: You'd like to know what value there is in using the process?

Q: That would help, I guess.

A: You're still unsure. Let's use our conversation so far as an example of why affective reflection is valuable.

Q: Okay.

A: When you said you felt phony using it and that "maybe it's just not me," what if I had said to you, "Yep. Some people feel that way." How would you have felt?

Q: I don't know. Maybe like you could care less how I felt about it.

A: What if I had said, "Well, it's been proven that they're effective." What then?

Q: That sounds a little argumentative, to be honest.

A: Uh huh…

Q: Or condescending. Like you know everything, and I don't because you're the expert, and I can't see why they're necessary.

A: (Quiet and nodding head in agreement).

Q: So…..why use them?

A: The reason I think affective reflections help is that when we're talking with someone who feels emotional about something, they give us a way to understand more about what the person is trying to communicate and continue the conversation. It's so easy to steamroll over someone and shoot back our opinion, tell them what we think, or change the subject, rather than offering to listen. And it's very easy to do this with kids. In doing so, we risk shutting down communication or having them go away feeling disrespected, one-upped, resentful, or uncared for. There's empathy involved in acknowledging how someone is feeling about something, in trying to understand their perspective.

Q: I can appreciate all that but it's still not easy to do.

A: It can seem hard, to begin with. It takes practice—and focusing on what the other person is saying before we jump in with our own "wisdom." After a while, it just seems a natural way to let others know that you're truly interested in what they're saying to you and that you care enough about them to want to talk about it.

Q: We just enrolled our son in what we thought would be a really good preschool. It had been recommended to us by several neighbors whose own children had attended it. They say it still has a great reputation, but we're wondering if we made a mistake. We thought he needed it before going to kindergarten because he's not very interested in having us read to him or learning his numbers. All he wants to do is play with his friends, and it seems that's a lot of what they do at his school. The teacher does read to them every day, and they do these little projects and small groups that he gets excited about, but we thought it would be more academic. The school does advertise that they have a "play-based" curriculum. What is that? And should we be looking around for a better fit for him (and us)?

A: You may have stumbled on a gold mine without realizing it. Make an appointment with the teachers to talk about what's involved in the school's play-based curriculum in terms of early learning and development. That could vary from school to school, but it usually involves the teacher developing a theme or project based on the children's interests (ex. A restaurant, airport, store, doctor's office). Children adopt culturally based roles and through their play, they learn the rules, use tools, and develop the skills associated with adult-world activities. While the children's work is not based on a prescriptive syllabus, it is hardly laissez-faire and will be intentionally directed at having the children grow academically and developmentally. Make time to observe what goes on for a morning in the classroom. If the school really is as good as your neighbors have suggested, you may be surprised. Play is a significant influence in all aspects of children's lives— cognitive, physical, and social. As you watch what's going on, look for the following as children play with one another: collaboration, negotiation, problem solving, communication, imagination and creativity, flexibility in behavior and thinking, sharing, resolution of conflicts, leadership, following the leader, and playing by the rules. Those are the gold nuggets of play. All of this provides opportunities for new competencies to be explored, modified, practiced, or even discarded for more effective strategies.[37] It's been said that play is "big thinking in a child-friendly way," that it's a necessity and not a luxury.[38]

Red Flags That Signal Parenting Problems

1. Making children talk about their feelings when they don't want to.

2. Accusing children, using negative words *(ex. nasty, stubborn, greedy, manipulative)*.

3. Paying attention only to negative emotions and taking positive ones for granted.

4. Telling a child that his/her feelings are bad or denying them (ex. "You shouldn't be so angry. That's not nice." "Don't pay any attention to those kids. We love you, and that's all that counts.").

5. Children or parents who hide their emotions or resort to drugs or alcohol to cope with difficult emotions; prenatal exposure to tobacco (including marijuana), alcohol, and illicit drugs.

6. Children or parents who act inappropriately to show how they feel (ex. throwing or breaking things; hurting self or others; screaming; swearing).

7. Neglect.

8. Difficult temperaments that go unmodified; poor goodness-of-fit between parent and child.

9. Children who lack empathy for others or show no emotion in situations where they would be expected to.

10. Failure to acknowledge traumatic life events (death of a parent, serious accidents, racism, low socioeconomic exposure) or provide additional support that is needed.

What's in Your Parenting Toolkit?

1. Naming children's emotions and pointing out things that prompt them.

2. Using affective reflections to help children understand what they're feeling.

3. Talking about your own feelings in various situations, using a variety of feeling words.

4. Asking children to name another child's feelings.

5. Using narrative picture books to prompt discussion with children about emotions.

6. Using lots of different feeling words over time (ex. delighted, annoyed, embarrassed, fearful) in addition to the primary ones (happy, mad, sad, and afraid).

7. Teaching the value of optimism and modeling it.

8. Teaching children friendship skills.

9. Coaching children in decision making, planning, implementing, and evaluating.

10. Fostering self-efficacy and self-determination by providing genuine, effective, and helpful feedback and acknowledging a child's problem-solving attempts and successes.

Conclusion

Without stable emotional development, our children cannot be successful in building a satisfying, rewarding life with others. In their earliest years, children need at least one adult who cares deeply about them. As they grow toward adolescence and adulthood, they need authoritative guidance that is accepting of differing temperaments and personalities but encourages children to develop self-regulation, a moral sense of right and wrong, and socially acceptable ways to get what they want and need. It is the kind of support that allows children to form the emotional intelligence, executive function, resilience and stress hardiness that will see them through the challenges they are sure to encounter as they traverse a complex world.

CHAPTER 3

Raising Socially Competent Children

We all have certain personality assets or deficits that influence our daily social interfaces with others. Children initially pick them up inside the family and then modify them in one way or another as they broaden their interactions with others.

When parenting has been overly protective, permissive, or punitive, appropriate social behavior is predictably more difficult for kids. However, if a reasonably sturdy foundation has been laid in the first several years for emotional stability, self-regulation, resilience, and strong executive functioning, they come fairly well equipped for the tasks involved in developing social competency. In our culture, that means they must become self-reliant, responsible, make good decision for themselves and others, and be honest, kind, and fair in their dealings with others.

In this chapter, our focus will be on how you can foster those kinds of worthy virtues in your children. Also included will be a concentration on how to help them develop prosocial behavior and friendships, deal with any aggressive behavior and bullying from others, transact the rapid social changes related to technology, and acquire healthy attitudes toward diversity and sexuality—all the elements of social competence.

Right from the Beginning: Building Self-Efficacy, Self-Determination and Responsible Behavior

Independence and responsibility are defining characteristics that take time and patience to cultivate in young children. In this arena, children have two major tasks: to learn to take care of themselves and to care for their environment. That takes the development of good, "figuring-it-out" intellectual functioning, such as planning ability and flexibility, being able to think for themselves, and becoming smart enough to ask for help when they need it. They need to develop analytic habits of thinking about how well their problem solving is going and gain insight into ways they can make things go differently when necessary.[39]

So—how do we help them with this? Authors Janet Gonzalez-Mena and Dianne Widmeyer Eyer note that human beings aren't born with social skills that just unfold as do gross motor or language skills. They have to learn what's valued and special to the culture from which they come, and they can only learn that from other people in their culture.[40]

Picture this: The Smiths and the Johnsons are relatives and have spent every Thanksgiving together for the past 8 years, alternating between the Smith and Johnson homes. The Smiths have three children, 7, 9, and 12. The Johnsons have two children, ages 8 and 10. Once dinner is over, the Smith children automatically begin to help clear the table; the Johnson children split to find a TV set to play their video games. The Johnsons notice that the Smith children are helpful, but they make no attempt to ask their own children to help. This is always true, no matter whether Thanksgiving is held at the Smith or Johnson home. To make matters worse, when the holiday dinner is held at the Smith's home, neither of the Johnson adults offer to contribute anything in the way of food or clean-up. This year, Mr. and Mrs.

Smith are weighing the benefits vs. irritations of getting together and considering terminating their long-standing get-together with the Johnsons.

This is not a case of "good kids" or "bad kids," but perhaps it is indicative of what the Smith and Johnson children have learned from their parents so far about being in the world. The Johnson children are comfortable with having others contribute to their well-being without necessarily having to reciprocate in any way whatsoever. The Smith sibs have developed a sense that they share responsibility for at least offering to help clean up after enjoying a meal someone has prepared for them.

There is no guarantee, of course, that the Smith children will always make better decisions and be more responsible than the Johnson children; but as these children grow older, the potential outcome becomes more predictable and even more stable. Out of the brief scenario above, here are clues that might suggest this:

- The Smith parents clearly model behaviors they want to see in their children.

- The Smith children have internalized the need to be helpful with occasional reminders from their parents if necessary.

- While the Johnson parents see more positive behaviors in other children, they lack the will to require them of their own children.

- The Johnson children have internalized that getting from others is far more satisfying than giving to others.

When you think about people you enjoy being with, they are usually those who carry a fair share of social responsibility. Whether it's contributing equitably to a conversation or trading off plans for social activities or just being someone who can be relied on when needed, favorite people "bring something to the table." They don't just take from and depend on others.

Some children are capable of finding all kinds of ways to ward off taking responsibility: There's the child who pretends (or actually comes to believe it) that he or she is incompetent: "I can't do this." "It's too hard." "I'm not smart like the other kids!" Another child strikes out at parents: "You're ruining my life." "I wish I had Katelyn's mother!" "I hate living in this house. You're SO mean!" Still another throws a tantrum until parents join the meltdown and give in or lash out in anger.

When parents fall into these traps because they allow their children to push their emotional buttons, guilt, anger, fear, anxiety, and discomfort can get in the way of teaching children to be independent and responsible. The result is that those children win the battle but lose in terms of life perspectives, skills, and capabilities. Unfortunately, this often reinforces laziness, a sense of entitlement, an overblown sense of self, or an internal sense of incompetency and dependency. Negative messages (voiced or unvoiced) are repeated over and over to the child: "You can't do this without my help." "You're incapable and inadequate." "No wonder you don't have any friends!" No well-meaning parent verbally sends these messages out loud to a child; however, when we take over a task because they aren't doing it well enough or quickly enough— or we accept excuses for irresponsible behaviors or demean them, we maintain children's dependency and deter growth.

Effective transmission of independence and the taking of responsibility is contingent on children having adults in their life who have appropriate expectations of what a child can and should be able to do, set limits in a non-punitive way, actively teach cooperation and kindness toward others, and offer lots of opportunities for a child to experience the good feeling that come from successful accomplishment of self-care and other tasks. Following are 5 essentials for supporting self-efficacy, self-determination, and responsible behavior in your children:

1. **Have appropriate expectations.** Expectations must be age-appropriate, with parents expecting neither too little nor too much. Sometimes, you might be confused about this, but there are many good sources to check out what children might be expected to do at any particular age and how to get them to do it (for example, Cecilia Decker's 8th edition of *Child Development: Early Stages through Age 12* and the excellent child development books written earlier by Frances Ilg and Louise Bates Ames).[41,42] Individual and some gender differences should always be taken into consideration, but a good rule of thumb is that if a child *can do* something alone or with help, the child should be expected to cooperate and behave in a way that's helpful to himself and to others as needed. Children should not be compared with other children, and their early attempts may be clumsy or not the end result you want, but be patient. Here's where your encouragement and opportunities for practice will be valuable. Undue criticism or taking over the task "so it can be done right" isn't helpful and usually results in resentment in a child and a poor learning trajectory.

2. **Teach your children the power of being effective decision makers and support the development of executive functioning.**[43] This starts very early with giving them as many choices as possible during the day (ex. "Should we put away all the large blocks first or the small ones?" "We need to water the plants and feed the fish. Which do you want to do?" "What'll

it be for lunch today—a peanut butter sandwich or grilled cheese?" "Let's get these dishes done. Do you want to wash or wipe?" "It's better to make a plan about getting that homework done and stick to it. It's up to you: always after school or always after dinner?"). Make sure that if you give them a choice, you'll be willing to accept the one they opt for and won't negate it. Then, have children take responsibility for the choice they make. For example, if your daughter has chosen to do homework after dinner instead of after school but then wants to watch a favorite TV show she's forgotten about after dinner, have her stay with her choice and follow through, even if there are tears and pouting. Finally, without moralizing or judging, encourage children to evaluate their own decisions by asking later on if things turned out as they had planned and, if not, what they would do differently the next time.

3. **Set clear boundaries.** Figure out where you want your children's decision making to start and end. They shouldn't have complete freedom to do whatever they want and should know clearly what the limits are, particularly when they're very young, inexperienced, or involved in something that could be unsafe or unhealthy. As they grow older, they'll be more capable of making serious decisions; however, having complete freedom to make all of their own decisions is too much responsibility and stressful. Your children should always know that without being inflexible or insensitive, you are open to talking with them about what they want to do and will be supportive unless a possible outcome would be unsafe or detrimental.

4. **Model desired behaviors.** This is where you set up a

family "code of conduct" and actively teach qualities you want to see in your children. Children naturally imitate what they see. That's how they learn. For example, when you help a neighbor with something or return something you've borrowed on time, they're watching. When you call a friend just to see if she's all right or volunteer in your child's school, at church, or in the community, they're noticing. When someone does something nice for you and you thank them and "return the favor," they're more likely to emulate that kind of behavior themselves later on. You can also verbally point out behaviors in others, coaching your children to pick up on details they might not notice otherwise, such as when someone is resisting temptation or delaying gratification: "Looks like Sarah's waiting to use the computer, but she's waiting patiently. That's good. Let her know when you've finished." If they fail to notice that someone has gone out of the way to help them or please them and haven't acknowledged it, remind them to do so: "Your sister worked hard on making that birthday card for you. She wanted it to be special. Make sure you thank her for it." "You're enjoying that gift Yaya and Papa sent. Let's send them a thank you note. They'll enjoy getting it." Modeling and coaching are two very essential ways to help children recognize and internalize self-regulation and positive behavior toward others.

5. **Be careful not to be overprotective or allow children to dodge responsibility.** Remember that children learn by being able to suffer reasonable consequences when they make unwise decisions, fail to take responsibility, or treat others badly. When you're overprotective or neglect to redirect your child's behavior because you're

worried it'll affect your relationship in a negative way, the result can be serious flaws in their development. That can include your children not developing empathy for others or conscience, not understanding cause-and-effect in their interactions with others, and immature or unrestrained behavior. Poor self-esteem is the ultimate penalty because others won't like them or want to be around them, and they won't like themselves very much either.

Growing independent and responsible children is sometimes like being a good coach. You stay on the sidelines and patiently teach the skills—little by little—that you know your child will need in order to become socially competent. You then step aside as soon as you can and, where appropriate, you watch them try it themselves. You realize there's no replacement for practice, and you know that when learning a skill, your child may backslide at times and need additional guidance to get to a point where he or she has internalized a particular skill and that the skill has become automatic. For example, once we have become fully accustomed to washing our hands after using the bathroom, we have an internal mechanism that routes us automatically toward the sink before leaving the bathroom. We are no longer dependent on our parents or some other adult to keep us healthy in that respect and are responsible for our own welfare.

Prosocial Behavior and Friendship Building

When we're kind or help others, share what we have, or defend or comfort someone when they need it, our feelings of satisfaction, usefulness, competence, and happiness are predictably at their highest. Prosocial behavior, which is voluntary and aimed at being helpful to others in some way,[44] has all kinds of benefits that we want for our children. It is the basis for a lifelong ability to form and keep good relationships. Without it, children are less likely to have friends and more likely to be seen as selfish, antisocial, or overly dependent. Conversely, when they've developed prosocial traits, they are more apt to be popular with others, welcome in others' social spheres, and better able to gain cooperation and help from others when they need it.

Because human beings are social creatures, we know that prosocial behavior has biological underpinnings, that all human societies value it, and that parents, peers, and the media are influential in moderating it.[45] At its core, it can be as simple as a child sharing a toy with a friend or at its most sophisticated, something like the late Martin Luther King, Jr. and Congressman John Lewis's commitment toward advancing civil rights.

When children exhibit prosocial behavior, it's not always easy to know what's motivating it. What we do know is that it is shaped by a child's age, empathic ability to think of and help others, an understanding of right and wrong, and experiences with watching such behavior by others and what results from it. It may be done without any thought of reward in mind and only because a child feels empathic toward what someone else needs. That's the best scenario. Sometimes, however, there's an ulterior motive, and it's simply to put themselves in a better position to get what they want. Children who can be described as prosocial believe that if they're polite, cheerful, cooperative, and helpful, their peers and teachers will like them better—and they're right. Also, they're likely to repeat prosocial behavior to keep on getting those affirmative responses. Some may be influenced by people they see as heroic or morally inspirational. For whatever reason, when your children choose to be prosocial, it heavily influences their social competence and chances for ongoing, positive relationships with others.

For children to act in a prosocial manner, they have to be able to tune in to others' needs. They do that by accurately interpreting others' facial expressions, words, and body language. Parents help children who don't yet have this awareness when they point out someone's need for help and ways in which it is signaled. How children respond depends on whether they see themselves as *able* to be helpful, their relationship to the person in need of help, and their desire to help. Parents help grow prosocial attributions when they say such things to a child as "You shared your orange with your sister because you like to make others happy." "You were really helpful right now when Martin couldn't find his tennis shoes and you showed him where you saw them." Children may want to help but not know what they can do in certain situations. This is where parents can assist by offering options ("You could write a card for Karl to cheer him up or call him on the telephone. I think he'd like either one.").

Sharing, which is a significant component in prosocial behavior, always comes up in parenting workshops—without fail. When we force children to share or require it, and it isn't voluntary, we can't really call it "sharing." With younger children who are fighting over an object, it helps to neutralize the object by removing it to a place nearby, laying a hand on it, and saying, "You both want to play with this. What can we do so you both have a chance?" Prompt each of them to make a suggestion. Repeat the suggestions ("You think you had it first. Kevin thinks he should just have it. What do you both think of that?"). Stay neutral and don't show any disapproval or label one of the children's suggestion in a negative way, even if it's unreasonable. Remind them that if they're going to get the object back, they have to come up with a fair way so that both get a turn and agree to it. If they get stymied, offer some alternatives ("You could each get something else to play with or you could take turns with this. How would you do that?"). If they refuse to cooperate in the process, don't solve it for them; just put the object away. However, if a solution has been reached, praise them for coming up with one and then make sure they follow through on what they've decided. This takes time, but it's teaching your children how to be cooperative and advance their prosocial behavior. Eventually, they'll realize that they can initiate the process themselves without getting you involved, and that's what you want.

You can also reinforce sharing among young children by pointing out instances of sharing when they happen, reading stories that illustrate it and then talking about it, and giving them scripts to ask for something. For example, 3-year-old Kelsey has a tendency to grab what she wants from her 5-year-old brother or complaining to you and asking you to intervene. Tell her, "You want the red crayon, and Caleb's using it. Grabbing just makes him angry. Ask him, 'Caleb, may I have that red crayon as soon as you're finished?'). When she does so, say, "Caleb, Kelsey has asked nicely about using the red crayon when you're finished. Let her know when you're done with it."). Talk with Caleb privately about reinforcing this process himself if his younger sister reverts to grabbing or whining by reminding her to ask for what she wants. This teaches both children more about prosocial behavior and effective communication. Kelsey has a better idea of how to ask for what she wants, and Caleb's perspective-taking skills and understanding of prosocial behavior are increased, making it more likely that he'll independently use the skills himself.

True sharing or voluntarily giving up something usually improves between the ages of 6 and 12 because of children's developing intellectual reasoning and language abilities, greater ability to see others' perspectives, their desire for acceptance and approval from others, and their sense of fairness and justice ("We take turns, right?"). They move from self-oriented rationales for sharing ("He'll like me better if I share.") to other-oriented reasons ("She'll feel better if I give her a turn."). They also make the transfer from concrete reasoning ("It's mine and I don't have to share it.") to more abstract values ("Everyone feels better if they get to use it.").[46]

In working actively to increase your child's prosocial behavior, be careful to avoid the following pitfalls:

- **Failing to recognize your child's efforts to be helpful to another** when they sometimes don't go so well. For example, your older child pours a younger one's juice and spills juice all over the table. It doesn't help to say, "You've made a mess. You need to think before you do things." Instead, it would be better to acknowledge the older child's intentions: "You were trying to help. That pitcher was too heavy. Help me clean up the juice."

- **Making unfavorable comparisons between one child's considerate behavior and another's lack of it.** A detrimental statement might be: "Simon, Henry plays quietly while I'm on the phone. Why can't *you* do that?" It would be more positive to thank Henry for playing quietly while you're on the phone and let it go at that, "Henry, thank you for playing quietly while I was on the phone. That was helpful." Simon will notice.

- **Coercing children to participate in insincere prosocial behavior.** There are many different versions of this. Most frequently seen are adults who force children to say they're sorry when they don't really mean it. When this happens, kids learn that saying "sorry" fixes everything and that insincerity makes their unacceptable behavior okay—that they can do whatever they want to, just as long as they say they're sorry. Instead, parents should look for some way to have children make restitution for a wrongdoing and only encourage them to say they're sorry if they appear to have genuine remorse for something they've done.

- **Making children share everything all the time.** (Ex. William is practicing his free throws with the family's basketball and his brother Robert is complaining that he wants to take the ball down to the nearby playground to play with some friends, that his brother has had it "all morning." You hear his brother say, "Not now. I need to keep practicing for the game tomorrow." Ignoring that, you remind them that the rule is to share and then arbitrarily legislate turn-taking of the ball by telling William that he has 10 more minutes to use the ball and then has to share it with his brother). Here's where parents cause resentment, usually resulting in neither child being satisfied. Instead, you could ask William if he'd be willing to let Robert have it for a while if he has time to continue practicing later on. If he agrees, praise him for doing so. If he declines, accept his decision to do so and suggest that Robert might call one of his friends to see if someone else can bring a basketball.

Guiding children's prosocial development will have a lot to do with the kind of relationship you've established with them, the extent to which you've used authoritative strategies to parent, behaviors you model, and ways in which you acknowledge and reward helpful and cooperative behaviors.

As children spend more and more time outside the family circle, the prosocial behaviors they've already learned with you will be valuable in developing peer relationships and friendships. Peers are commonly age-mates kids spend time with during school, sports, and religious activities. Beyond that, they may not spend large amounts of time with one another. From their interactions with peers, children learn a great deal in terms of self-regulation, prosocial behavior, cultural differences, and understanding of where they fit in the social world. They pay attention to what it takes to be a leader or a follower, sometimes experimenting with one role or another, and pick up an amazing list of skills from one another:[47]

- Starting conversations
- Inviting others to play and responding to play invitations
- Using a not too loud nor too quiet voice
- Matching facial expressions, body movements, and words
- Keeping a conversation going
- Answering another child's questions
- Expressing appreciation and affection
- Recognizing other people's feelings and needs
- Waiting and taking turns
- Following game rules
- Sharing materials
- Offering to help and comfort
- Listening to other people's ideas
- Suggesting ideas and making plans
- Resolving conflicts without hitting, hurting, or retreating
- Controlling angry outbursts
- Acknowledging mistakes and excusing others' mistakes

Children can run into difficulty in peer relationships if they are excessively shy and passive or overly aggressive. In the first case, they can become neglected by peers and increasingly isolated because they have few skills in attracting other children's attention in socially acceptable ways, fewer prosocial skills, and trouble entering a play group. When aggressive or socially awkward, a child may be rejected or avoided by peers and when this happens, they can either become more aggressive or withdrawn depending on their personalities.[48]

Friendships are quite different than peer relationships. The bonds that develop between a child and a close friend are stronger, definitely more special, and much more personal. They enjoy spending as much time together as possible and feel affectionate toward one another or upset when the other one is upset. They choose to be together because they feel cared for and secure when together, not because they are required to spend time with one another as happens in school with peers. The relationship between a child and a true friend offers much deeper give-and-take. They share their perceptions about people and life, openly express their opinions and ideas, and are interested in what the other one thinks about the same things. The alliance allows each child a greater self-awareness, the chance to refine their prosocial skills and build trust, work out problems with one another, argue, and still remain friends. This all sets the stage for how they are likely to handle subsequent close relationships as they grow toward adulthood.

Children are not born knowing how to build peer relationships or how to make and keep friends. As children are learning how to be social, they can misread cues from others, act in aggressive ways, be uncooperative, act silly and show off, or display immature behavior. Those who are most likeable and sought out by their peers are those who express interest in others by establishing eye contact, smiling, nodding, and asking questions of other children. They take turns, share, and listen to others' ideas. They often express affection by spontaneously hugging, holding hands, or asking another child to "be friends." They are empathic when they see someone who's sad or needs help, try to offer help when needed, and praise other children when they have a good idea or do something well.[49]

Children are attracted to others because of similarity in physical appearance, ethnicity, gender, age, behavior characteristics, abilities, interests and attitudes, executive function, and social competence.

When children are having trouble making friends, there are three essential things they will need help with: 1) appropriate friend behavior; 2) friendship-related skills and how to use them; and 3) how to modify their behavior while interacting with peers. Without those skills, they are unlikely to develop and keep a friendship for very long.

Parents can provide a form of social skills training for their children. This might involve helping them better recognize friendly overtures of others and how to respond more appropriately to them, understand how a particular behavior of theirs may annoy others, and learn the "language" of negotiation and compromise (ex. "I'm using this right now. You can have it in a minute."). Instead of overwhelming a child with all they may have to learn, choose just one friendship skill at a time to talk with them about. Tell them why it's important to learn that skill. Read children's books about particular ones, such as sharing or helping a friend and then talk about it. Role play with them and give them scripts for interacting when they need them. Talk with a professional who can help give you tips for promoting your child's friendship skills when you don't feel you or your child are making progress. The worst thing would be to ignore a child's unhappiness about not having any friends or inability to negotiate conflict with others. The best thing would be to recognize when children need help, to believe that children can be taught how to be a friend and make friends, to create play opportunities where you or a teacher can observe how well they're doing, and to coach them where they're having particular difficulty.

Aggressive Behavior and Bullying

It's not uncommon to see very young children being aggressive in their initial social interactions. They see something they want, and they haven't yet developed the prosocial behaviors they need in order to get it without being physically aggressive. In this case, they don't mean to hurt someone else on purpose. This is called *instrumental aggression*. We see it more often in toddlers and young children who have immature language skills and haven't developed socially acceptable strategies for attempting to get what they want.

A more serious form of aggression is when children intentionally harm another child by saying or doing something hurtful. *Hostile aggression* can be either physical by actually harming another person or threatening to do so. It's called *relational* when it is intended to damage someone's status or self-esteem.

There do appear to be some inherited links to aggression, such as male sex hormones and intense, boisterous, or distractible temperament. Frustration, a distorted perception of another child's intent and wanting to retaliate for it can cause a child to be seen as aggressive by other children and to be rejected or avoided because of it.

Aggression is different than being *assertive* where we're expressing ourselves or protecting our rights while still being relatively respectful to the other person. What we want to see in our children as they approach 5 and 6 years of age is the greater use of assertiveness to resist unreasonable demands or aggressive acts from another child, stand up against unfair treatment, and resolve conflicts in a peaceful way. By now, they should have somewhat greater impulse control, understanding of "rules" for interacting with others by "using their words," and problem-solving abilities.

As they move towards middle school, children's growing cognition and perspective-taking competence allows them to get better at resolving hostile or instrumental disputes; on the other hand, they also begin to believe that social wrongs or real and imagined slights by others deserve some sort of reciprocity or "revenge." During these years, you are likely to see less physical aggression but more hostile aggression in the form of insults, baiting, and rejection of others based on "getting even."

Practices by parents that can escalate children's aggressive behavior include ignoring it and hoping it'll just go away, using displacement strategies they've hear of such as encouraging children to hit a stuffed object or pillow when they're angry, or simply being firm one day and lax on another one because they're sick and tired of dealing with their child's negative behavior. The most damaging response to children's aggressive behavior is using physical punishment to "teach them how it feels." For example, this can be a parent who chooses to bite a young child who's been biting other children, pinch one who's been pinching, or one who uses other forms of corporal punishment intended to get a child's attention and keep her from "acting up." Biting or pinching by an adult might be temporarily effective in eliminating the child's biting or pinching but create larger problems. Studies by medical, psychology, and education scientists have proven that such approaches only teach children how to be more aggressive, that "might makes right," and that aggression is the best option for eliminating aggression. They also learn that parents are someone to be afraid of and not to be trusted and that they will have to work harder at not being caught for their aggression against others.[50]

What we want to do instead is to have our children internalize values and ways to interact with others that are wholly incompatible with violence, and the best way to do that is to make it clear to our children that aggression is never acceptable, to teach them how to meet their needs constructively, and educate them in appropriate ways to respond to the aggression of others. Practices that have proven effective in dealing with children's aggressive behavior include the following:

- Find ways to reduce their frustration; help them find constructive ways to deal with it.

- Help them interpret social situations more accurately.

- Stop them from hurting others or damaging property.

- Always use an alternative to corporal punishment such as logical and appropriate unrelated consequences when correcting aggressive behavior.

- Forbid aggression and follow-through on rules; never ignore it.

- Assist them in de-escalating aggressive play (for example, encourage them to be the "good and virtuous" superhero and not a vengeful, aggressive one.)

- Reinforce them for using non-aggressive problem-solving.

- Model caring, respectful behavior and respond to aggression calmly and rationally when you're dealing with conflict or frustrating situations with others. Remember that they learn by imitating how you react to those kinds of situations.

- Teach them how to better understand their emotions and those of others.

- Actively teach friendship skills, assertive communication skills, and alternatives to aggression.

- Teach them how to work through conflicts peaceably.[51]

The most extreme form of hostile aggression is *bullying* in which children deliberately exert power to hurt others. It's important to point out that not every mean thing that is done to or said about children by their peers can be defined as bullying. As they grow toward adolescence, there's a lot of joking around, shoving and pushing, name calling, humiliation, and exclusion that isn't bullying, and it's important for kids to be able to determine what the difference is and how to react to it. Sometimes, that's confusing.

Bullying clearly goes beyond aggression and crosses the line. It's malicious, and frequency matters. One-time assaults or acts are *not* bullying because they don't continue, whereas in bullying, a child is targeted again and again, there is an imbalance of power and intimidation, and there is always willful intent. It can be electronically texted, online, written, or in person.[52] Boys tend to use mostly physical assaults, and girls are more likely to hurt others by snarky remarks, exclusion, and other intentionally hurtful verbal or online strategies.

It's a myth that bullies most likely have poor self-esteem. Some do feel inferior and hide that while dominating others. However, the most common type of childhood bullies are those who truly feel superior to other children, enjoy using aggression to get what they want, and believe that their fearless, coercive, and impulsive behavior is not only justified but escalates them in the eyes of their peers. They come to enjoy the authority and clout they have over others. They may have experienced bullying themselves or live in homes where there are few rules or limits and where aggression is commonly used by one or more members of the family. Some are angry about the way they're forced to live or feel they have no one who really cares about them. Instead of confronting a neglectful or punitive caretaker, they find someone weaker among their peer group and take their resentment and rage out on that child. When bullying is allowed to continue, with no one challenging such children, they are more likely to be involved in delinquency by middle school and experience higher rates of academic failure. In adulthood, most fare even worse.

If you hear that your child is bullying someone else—no matter what the reason—act on it immediately. In no uncertain terms, tell him or her that it won't be tolerated. Follow through with needed consequences if it continues, keeping in mind they are every bit as vulnerable as their victims. Everyone suffers when bullying goes on.

Victims are usually kids who have trouble asserting themselves, lack language proficiency or communication abilities, and have serious deficiencies in social skills. They simply attract others' scorn. Temperament can play a role in this, since bullies like to pick on socially withdrawn, anxious, submissive and insecure children who are the least popular. They're usually kids who have few friends and are the least chosen for activities. They typically respond to the bullying passively, not standing up for their rights. Others provoke it by arguing ineffectively or crying easily. They're most likely to overreact to common joking and teasing, when other children better understand that it isn't meant to be offensive, and that may start the process. Often, when the bullying of a particular child in school has become chronic, and especially in later elementary, the child becomes the "goat" of a class, is looked on as weak and disliked by most classmates, and elicits little sympathy from anyone. Often, as other kids try to "fit in," they support the bully's behavior.

Witnesses to bullying are also affected, even if they are not directly involved. They see that bullies often get what they want and are even popular because of their bullying. They may feel guilty about not helping the victim but are afraid they'll end up being bullied themselves or may even join in on the bullying if others do. If they don't stand up for the child being bullied, they strengthen the bully's tendencies toward violence. It's important to let them know that if they do have the courage to defend the bully's prey and challenge the behavior, the aggression is more likely to end.

If your child is the target of a bully, do not leave him on his own to "work things out." It's likely that it's going to take adult intervention of some kind to deal with it. The greatest need victims usually have is to build their verbal assertiveness skills so they can protect their rights. They may need training in exactly what to say and practice in appearing more confident (even when they feel scared to death inside). If they have had trouble making friends, they need help with that as well because bullies are less likely to pick on someone who other children like. They may try to hide the chronic bullying from family members because they're ashamed of it, but helplessness, rejection, and unhappiness is likely something they'll experience every day. When children are averse to going to school or a center or playing in the neighborhood (bullying can happen to children as young as 3), not sleeping well, or acting out in aggressive ways themselves toward younger children or pets, it may be a possibility that they're facing some kind of bullying.

Here's another wrinkle. Child bullies now also use computers, smart phones, and I-pads to hide their victimizing from adults while still teasing, mocking, threatening, spreading nasty rumors, and calling other children names. Called *cyberbullying*, it should cause special concern because of its insidiousness, frequent anonymity, and the trauma it may cause. One child can be the target, receiving the destructive messages, or the perpetrator can increase the damage by sending missives to a wider audience, such as an entire class, school, neighborhood, or community.

While bullying happens more often in middle schools than in elementary schools, it does happen with pre-teen children, with 1 in 4 children eventually being a victim during their school years and 1 in 6 children cyberbullying others.[53] It could be a once-only episode or it can go on for long periods of time, but there are emotional costs with both. When it continues, and the child can't handle it but doesn't seek help from a trusted adult, the consequences to the victim can be severe.

Kids often say they don't go to a parent or teacher about it because they fear the adult will overreact, get angry, or try to step in and resolve the problem themselves (sometimes, creating a bigger or more embarrassing problem).[54] Instead, the adult needs to listen and then remind the child about problem solving and conflict resolution skills they can use to handle the assault. That can range from simply blocking the cyberbully and cutting off all contact to reporting the victimizer to school authorities. Increasing numbers of schools have written policies for dealing with bullying, and expulsion is included. Certainly, schools are a likely place for bullying to take place, as well as a venue for dealing effectively with it and offering program-wide solutions for keeping children safe from it.

Because of the seriousness of cyberbullying, parents need to stay in close communication with their child if it happens, watching for any signs that the bullying is continuing or escalating and stepping in to provide additional support when needed. If the child seems nervous or upset after getting a call or computer/I-pad message, get a conversation going by offering an affective reflection, "You seem upset." or asking, "Are you okay?"

Other signs of cyberbullying include a child's increasing secrecy about online activity, withdrawal from family and friends, avoiding group activity and events, acting out at home, or making lower grades in school. There may be changes in appetite, mood, or sleep patterns. Mental health issues such as depression, anxiety, and even thoughts of suicide can result from all types of bullying; but, because cyberbullying often renders the victim with greater feelings of helplessness, the effects can be more severe and even life-threatening.

Handling the Risks and Opportunities of Technology

In an airport recently, I noticed a three-year-old and his parents sitting across from me, each of them with a hand-held device. All of them were completely absorbed in what they were doing, and no one spoke for the 45 minutes we waited until our flight was called. In the rows and rows of people waiting to board, almost everyone was engaged in some sort of technology. Similarly, those waiting in line were mostly silent, glued to something on a smart phone, and as they approached the agent, most of those under 50 showed their ticket on their phone instead of a paper one. As I boarded and made my way down the aisle, 90% of those already seated were engaged with a smart phone, computer, or I-pad, and we hadn't even taken off yet!

During the flight, I continued to think about the ubiquitous connections people have with screens and the diminishing amount of time spent interacting with non-screen human beings. Many of us now work from home, order groceries, clothing, books, and furniture on-line, and use it for entertainment and education (especially during the pandemic!). We Zoom, video, pay bills, check the weather and news, keep our calendars and scrapbooks of photos on it, and keep in touch with friends and family on Zoom, Facetime, Twitter, MySpace, and Facebook instead of in person. I wondered what all that meant for that 3-year-old "netizen"[55] I had just seen with his mesmerizing, non-human "playmate." How much did his parents understand about the risks and opportunities involved in his early love affair with technology?

There's no one today who would deny that becoming techno-literate is a requirement for a 21st century education. It just is. The rapid, unrelenting shift toward the use of technology in our everyday lives is no less important that what happened in the 15th

century with Gutenberg's invention of the printing press, and we can't even begin to imagine what's ahead in the future.

Yet, there are concerns, and while child development professionals and policymakers have said that parents and teachers should guard against the harm it can do, children's early and very savvy involvement in technology has already outpaced research and put inordinate pressure on parents to concede early and sometimes imprudent immersion.

The American Academy of Pediatricians recommends no screen time at all for children eighteen months of age and younger and only 1-2 hours daily of monitored use after that. They also suggest that parents limit screens in favor of encouraging reading and turn screens off to give play a chance.[56] Seventy percent of families ignore these proposals because the lure of children being kept entertained and occupied via technology is just too great. Also, many take pride in their child's know-how with technology and see it as necessary for a competitive future. If you're an average family, your children are spending about 5 ½ hours per day or more on entertainment screens, such as TV, video games, social networks, and online videos. Teenagers spend an additional 2 ½ hours texting and talking on the phone. Seventy percent of parents allow texting during meals.[57] Check it out.

Most parents are trying to find a balance between embracing the blitz and resisting it. Many admit that they teeter between being too lazy or too permissive to challenge a child's overuse versus being too strict or inflexible. Many are unsure about how much time their children *should* be spending with technology, what they should be watching or not watching, and how to keep them from getting involved in online activity that might be harmful. Neuroscientists are studying how technology impacts on the wiring of young, developing brains. Both parents and teachers share their fears that it may be negatively affecting overall socialization, since it takes away from face-to-face play and gives children the illusion of companionship without the demands created from building and maintaining real friendships.[58] Some are dealing with the cyberbullying discussed in the previous section and its potentially damaging effects on their child's emotional well-being.

The upside is that technology does offer our children the following:

- Greater access to an unending store of audio-visual information and knowledge, world-wide, as well as greater motivation to access it
- Expanded forms of literacy ("new" literacies that have resulted from technology such as text messaging, blogging, video making, emailing, social networking)
- A wide variety of entertaining learning tools to practice skill building (ex. mathematics and language games online)
- Diverse skill building in many forms of techno-literacy to keep up with society's unremitting investment, involvement, and interest in technology
- A possible increase in attentional skills
- Access to additional entertainment venues
- Social give-and-take skills required in playing video games with another person
- Online outlets for creative play, such as environments or objects to move around, refashion, and manipulate.[59]

Current research indicates that there's also a downside for many children, including the following:[60]

- Inappropriate usage can negatively affect a child's emotional health, school performance, and later chances of success. Studies have indicated that heavy usage among adolescents and college students predicts low academic accomplishment, but those online behaviors are built in childhood.

- It may lead to phone compulsion and/or screen addiction.

- There is often a distancing, reconfiguring effect on the family, especially between children and parents, as each person focuses on his own computer, TV set, or other device and often in separate rooms.

- There is a negative effect on self-control and increased impulsive or covert behavior.

- As a child's life becomes saturated with media, there is a decrease in non-digital activity with peers and family members.

- Imagination and abstract thinking that is normally developed during play in early childhood is reduced.

- Higher rates of obesity are resulting from a lack of physical activity and snacking while viewing.

- There is increased vulnerability to cyberbullying, sexting behaviors, and exposure to alcohol, tobacco use, and sexual behaviors, resulting in the possibility of earlier initiation of these behaviors.[61, 62]

When taking a proactive parental approach to monitoring children's interaction with all forms of technology, both personal responsibility and judgment have to be exercised by both parents and children. Following are some ideas that may keep your child safer:[63]

1. Educate yourself about cyberbullying, chat rooms, gaming sites and other potentially problematic or dangerous online sites that your children can get into.

2. Create a media plan for your family and be very clear about screen-time rules. Make sure all of them are reasonable and enforceable. Share this plan with others who may be caring for your children (ex. babysitters and grandparents) so that everyone's aware of what you want. Be consistent about follow-through and corrective consequences when rules are violated.

3. Get to know the parents of your children's friends. Talk with them about any rules they have for their children relative to internet and screen usage, since your children will have access to anything their friends' parents allow when visiting. Share your family rules with them.

4. Talk with your children about what you expect from them and be honest about your concerns. Listen to what they think about usage. Tell them you expect them to be accountable and want to trust them with the responsibility to maintain safe online behaviors, such as never interacting with people they don't know.

5. When appropriate, talk with them about sexting and predators who may use social networking, chatrooms, email and online games to contact and exploit children. The American Academy of Pediatrics reports that twelve percent of children 10-19 years of age have posted nude or seminude images of themselves and/ or explicit messages online. Make sure children know that whatever they post online may be permanent and ultimately open for anyone to view forever.

6. Use parental control apps that block certain websites you don't want them to have access to at all and self-control apps that you expect them to use independently to block certain websites at certain periods of time (for example, when they're supposed to be doing homework or after a certain hour in the evening).

7. To ward off nocturnal social networking and online visits, have children put their phones and I-pads in a particular place at a certain time (ex. on the kitchen counter or on your bedroom dresser before bedtime). If a child doesn't respect the rule, give a warning and then lock up the devices overnight if necessary.

8. Insist on at least one hour of non-screen activities each day, as well as a time limit for overall usage; taper excessive screen time when you see it's necessary and limit access completely when necessary.

9. Have a separate computer to do just schoolwork if possible.

10. Have a central location for TVs in your home, children's computers, and game consoles. Have them in a place where you're naturally and frequently present. They should not be in children's bedrooms. Check occasionally in a casual way to see what they're involved in watching or writing.

11. Use children's literature and videos about screen use to foster discussion with them about the safe use of technology. Following are some examples:
    - Alber, D. (2020). *A Little SPOT Stays Home: A Story about Viruses and Safe Distancing.*
    - Anton, C. and Lewis, S. (2017). *A Smart Girl's Guide: Digital World: How to Connect, Share, Play,*

– *and Keep Yourself Safe.*

– Bauer, S. C. & Sinclair, R. (2020). *Cami and Wyatt have Too Much Screen Time: A children's book that encourages imagination and family time.*

– Cook, J. & Hyde, M. H. (2013). *But It's Just a Game.*

– Cullinine, K. (2018). *Clicker the Cat*: Online children's book about internet safety, Ages 6-8.

– Herman, S. (2019). *Limit Your Dragon's Screen Time: Help Your Dragon Break His Tech Addiction.*

– Nhin, M. (2020). *Unplugged Ninja: A children's book about technology, screen time, and finding balance.*

– Rothfield-Kirschner, L (2019). *How We Got Cyber Smart: A Book about Staying Safe Online.*

Questions Parents Ask

Q: Getting our 9-year-old to do her homework every evening has become an ongoing hassle in our family. We've had her tested, and she doesn't have any learning disabilities, but we're worn out trying to get her to do what she clearly needs to do. We can't just let her fail, but she's got us over a barrel. No matter what we do, she refuses to take responsibility. It's exhausting! Any advice?

A: Without knowing what you've already tried, I'm not exactly sure what you're up against but it's clear that she's got the upper hand and shouldn't have. I suspect you've already tried sharing your honest concerns with her about this, your reasons about why it's important for her to take responsibility, and that it's her job and not yours to take care of what's become an aggravating problem. Start over. Make a reasonable plan with her about a specific time frame each afternoon or evening for homework and a place to do it (not in her bedroom). Tell her that you will ask her teacher to communicate with you each Friday about whether or not she's carefully completed each night's homework during the week. Give your daughter a clear warning about what will happen if she chooses not to be responsible. That means that she needs to observe the time frame and place that's been decided on without having to be reminded and that the teacher's report on Friday is a positive one. The consequence should be one that will make an impact on her, such as no screen time of any kind, including use of her phone, I-pad, TV, or computer (other than for homework) for the entire weekend and grounding so that she can't access anything at a friend's house. No matter what, follow through. That's the important part in making this work. If you're not consistent in doing that or if she can talk you out of any part of that, your plan will fail. If she argues, give her a warning and an additional consequence if it continues. Above all, stay calm. That's not easy to do in a situation like this, but it's absolutely necessary. Tell her everything starts all over on Monday. Then, allow her to take responsibility. That would mean not reminding her about the time frame or place, not hovering over her to make sure she's on task, not doing any part of her homework for her or checking to see if it's done correctly (that's the teacher's job), and continuing to get good reports from her teacher. Praise her when you see that she's turned the situation around and eliminated the hassle. If it becomes a problem again, immediately reinstitute the same plan.

Q: I think I'm over-worrying about this whole thing but am also curious about what my 11-year-old is doing on Facebook, her smart phone, and other online sites. She wants to have her own password and has asked for privacy. I'm a little tempted to snoop. Should I?

    A: No. There is a difference, however, between spying and monitoring. Spying would be prying without her knowledge. Monitoring is letting her know what you're doing and why you need to systematically review what's going on—just to keep her safe. When kids think their parents are spying or snooping, they have a tendency to go underground—and they often can because most kids today are far more knowledgeable about technology than are their parents. For example, some establish secret Facebook or App accounts that parents know nothing about. You do need to check what she's doing online and on social media, but you need to be up front with her. Tell her that you're going to be using a parental monitoring system that excludes sites that are not safe. There are a number of software possibilities that you can review, including K9 Web Protection, Norton Online Family, and Net Nanny. Find one that suits your comfort level. For children under 12, they can get along just fine with a flip phone that doesn't allow access to online activity. Be a "friend" on her social media site and let her know that she isn't to download any apps without your permission. You can check out the content of 70 or more of those by going to smartsocial.com.[64]

Q: I'm almost ashamed to admit this, but I just found out that my son and two other kids in his 4th grade class have been making fun of a classmate who has something called Tourette Syndrome. I told him his teacher had called, saying that they were actually making life miserable for a boy named Andrew by calling him names, mocking him, and excluding him on the playground. I was really disturbed when he said "No one likes him, Mom. He's just a creepy kid. He makes all kinds of stupid noises in class all day long, and he sniffs and barks like a dog." I told him I was disappointed in him and that it had to stop immediately. Other than that, I wasn't sure what else I could do.

A: Tourette's is a tough one for children who have it, particularly if it's severe. It usually starts in childhood, gets a little worse in adolescence and then, if they're lucky, it disappears before adulthood but not always. Because of faulty brain circuitry, there are uncontrolled vocal or motor tics. About 10-15% also have a condition called coprolalia where they'll blurt out socially unacceptable phrases or swear words or ethnic slurs. A lot of times, there are other developmental issues such as a learning disability and it's made worse when the child is under stress. These tics just happen and are almost impossible to suppress. What Andrew needs is to have his classmates understand what the condition is all about, that it's not something he can control, and that he wants to be treated like everyone else. This would be a good time for home and school to work together. Check with the teacher to see if she has let the class know about Tourette's and its symptoms. Go online with your son to learn more about the condition. Talk with him about how it would feel to have Tourette's and then have the additional burden of others making fun of something you can't control. Tell him that one thing he could do the next time he sees a classmate being unkind would be to have the courage to say something like "Knock it off. That's not funny. That's something he can't help." This is an excellent opportunity to have a discussion about the need to accept differences in other people and to stick up for someone who's being bullied instead of joining in. Let your son know that you're depending on him to be kind to other people. Acknowledge that sometimes that's hard when the gang is being hurtful to someone but that having a moral high ground is a powerful thing.

Q: This is something that really bothers me. When we have guests over for dinner and the evening, our kids come in at bedtime, give us a kiss, and say goodnight. So good, so far. But then, my husband always asks them to kiss our friends and tell them goodnight as well. I'm very uncomfortable with this, and it's obvious that the kids are as well because they always balk a little bit before doing what they've been asked, and that makes our guests uncomfortable. I've told my husband that a simple goodnight will do but he insists that he grew up this way and thinks it's just teaching them good manners.

A: The first word that pops into my head is "boundaries." Children definitely need to learn what boundaries are with respect to displaying affection for others, and they should never be coerced into kissing other people unless it's their choice and appropriate to do so. This is a time when it's not appropriate, since it makes others uncomfortable. A simple goodnight works. It fits the bill of being mannerly, which I agree is important, and teaching your children that they have rights with respect to showing affection. However, even more important here is that you've let your husband know you're not comfortable with something he's asking your children to do, and he still encourages them to do it. Although parents may continue to disagree about an issue, it's important for them to come to agreement about how to handle it in front of their children and support one another. Otherwise, kids can become confused and feel caught in a bind about what to do. They can also become manipulative, playing parents off against one another. When we're making decisions about our parenting based only on how "we grew up," there's always the chance sometimes that, with a little more thought, we can build a better mousetrap.

Q: Our daughter has just lost her best friend. They're almost seven now, and she and Laurie who lived next door had been playing together since they were preschoolers and then in the same class at school. The family moved out of state 3 weeks ago, and

Norah is just lost. She mopes around the house like a lost soul. I've encouraged her to invite another classmate home for a playdate, but she refuses to do so. Any suggestions?

A: This is a time when it's important to just listen when she's expressing sadness about her friend moving away. You can say, "You're missing Laurie. It's really hard that she's moved away. I'm sure that she's sad, too. Let's think of some ways that you girls can still connect with one another and stay friends." That could include emailing, talking with one another on the phone and using Facetime, sending a note to her in the mail, and sending a drawing or a picture. Talk with her teacher to see if members in the class can write a little note and offer to mail them all in a packet as a surprise. These kinds of losses take time to get over. While it's good to encourage her to find a new friend, don't push too hard. Once children know what it is to have a special friend, they usually make their way to a new one in their own time.

Red Flags That Signal Parenting Problems

1.   Children who seek inordinate attention (whether positive or negative), repeatedly express feelings of inadequacy, or display narcissistic qualities.

2.   Children who regularly exhibit a lack of responsibility for themselves or their environment.

3.   Parents who allow children complete freedom to make choices, argue with children, get into power struggles with them, or become psychologically or physically abusive.

4.   Failure or reluctance to follow through after giving a warning.

5.   Interfering in children's quarrels without giving them a chance to settle it them themselves.

6.   Ignoring aggression and bullying of any kind.

7.   Denying a child's perspective, taking sides, or laying blame when helping children solve a conflict.

8.   Failing to monitor technology usage and potential screen addiction in the family.

9.   Overreacting to children's normal or divergent sexual behavior, ignoring questions they have about their psychosexual development, or failing to intervene where behavior is not appropriate.

10. Family members making stereotypical remarks, jokes, references or negative slurs related to another person's sexuality or ethnicity.

What's in Your Parenting Toolkit?

1. Set realistic goals that consider your children's age, temperament, and abilities. Expect them to do everything they can do, fostering self-efficacy and self-determination.

2. Don't buy into excuses for irresponsible or attention-getting behavior. Apply corrective consequences and always follow through.

3. Realize your job is *not* to keep your children continually happy but to move them toward self-sufficiency.

4. Encourage friendship building by structuring play opportunities, helping your child recognize friendly overtures and behaviors in others, and coaching them where you see specific areas that need intervention, addressing only one skill at a time. Practice the skill with them.

5. Assist your children in conflict resolution by modeling and applying mediation in areas of conflict.

6. Use arguments and aggressive behavior as teachable moments about how to use assertive language instead of aggressive behavior.

7. Set limits on their use of technology. Be clear with your children about your expectations related to their observation of family rules, values, and morals.

8. Help your child understand the difference between an isolated hurtful action by someone and true bullying. Never ignore any evidence of bullying or cyberbullying by or against your child. Talk about ways to defend others who may be bullied.

9. Answer children's questions about sexuality honestly and handle sexual behavior such as masturbation, sex play, voyeurism, and LGBTQ issues as matter-of-factly as possible.

10. Examine your attitudes toward racial and ethnic diversity, knowing that they serve as an important prerequisite to producing or reducing stereotypical thinking and behavior in your children. Address stereotypical remarks directly and in a nonjudgmental manner, countering children's mistaken ideas.

Conclusion

There's little doubt that guiding children toward positive self-identity and social competency is a complicated, time-consuming, and labor-intensive task. You are the most important factor in whether your child will turn out to be a worthwhile human being who can make a positive contribution to the world or someone who may struggle lifelong with emotional instability and diminished self-efficacy and self-regulation. You will be the primary guide for your children, helping them learn what works and doesn't work in becoming socially adept and gradually attaining a mature level of competency. Of course, you'll share that responsibility with other influences in the child's world—grandparents, caregivers, teachers, religious leaders, neighbors, peers, and the media—but you will continue to serve as the closest observer, the most reliable confidante, and most caring change agent. It will be through you and with you that your child will develop the core life skills and positive attitudes toward others that are necessary for durable social competence.

CHAPTER 4

Helping Children Develop Healthy Attitudes toward Sexuality, Diversity, and Developmental Differences

You are unique from every other person you will ever meet in this world. When you were born, you came equipped with about 100 trillion cells that were organized into 20,000 to 25,000 units of heredity called genes that were then divided up into 23 pairs of chromosomes.[65] That is why, unless they are identical twins, your children will be different from one another in some ways and similar in others. Depending on genetics, they may favor either you or your husband physically and temperamentally (or resemble Grandpa or Aunt Martha more than either of you). It's all a roll of the dice! Added to those biological differences will be all the varied environmental influences and experiences that will further distinguish them from one another—and from you.

Family membership and belonging to certain ethnic, social, and cultural groups bring us closer together, based merely on the likenesses we share. Similarly, many of the differences we see in other people and groups cause us to reject them, based only on their beliefs, the color of their skin, their lifestyles and preferences, and certain behavioral and developmental characteristics. It all gets very complex, doesn't it? However, one thing is clear: Our children are not born with any particular likes or dislikes. As was sung in the play *South Pacific,* "You have to be carefully taught."

This chapter considers the biological underpinnings and characteristics related to differences in sexuality, ethnic diversity, developmental influences, and disabilities and the stereotypes, labels, and myths people attach to them. Also included is information about how our perspectives and those of others contribute to our children's developing social mindsets and behaviors.

Gender Identity and Sexuality

Our first understanding of ourselves and how we are different from or the same as someone else involves gender identity, that we are either male or female biologically. Between 3 and 6 years of age, we gain an understanding of the permanence of gender and that there are certain gender expression behaviors, such as toy preferences, dress, and mannerisms that are connected with and even expected of a particular gender. This strengthens and becomes more inflexible, particularly for boys, and there is evidence of stereotyping of interests, activities, and occupations that becomes quite rigid (ex. "Only women can be nurses." "Girls don't play hockey or football." "Only men can become firefighters and postal workers." "Boys can become President, but girls can't." "Boys who cry are sissies." "Mothers kiss hurts away but Daddies tell us to 'rub it in the dirt.'" "Daddies work and drive busses.").

This is a perfect age for parents to take advantage of some of the excellent picture books, chapter books, videos, and films that encourage children's broader understandings and attitudes toward gender-related behavior. It also helps if parents challenge stereotypical remarks directly and in a nonjudgmental manner by using open-ended questions ("Why do you think only women can become nurses?"), and then follow up with accurate information ("Some nurses are women; some nurses are men.").[66]

From infancy, all human beings experience sexual feelings, and they learn about sexuality just as they learn about everything else: through the words, actions, interactions, and relationships they have with significant others. As they develop, there may be sexual behaviors that are completely normal but cause parents concern, embarrassment, discomfort and uncertainty in how to handle them. For example, childhood masturbation is usually little more than self-soothing activity and is neither abnormal nor signaling precocious sexual behavior unless it goes on for a large part of a child's day. It can include rubbing genitals, sucking a thumb or fingers, stroking the edge of a blanket, or anything else that is comforting. Between the ages of 3-5, there can be overt emotional attachment to the opposite-sexed parent or a favorite adult, inappropriate sex play or peeping among children that should be *calmly* redirected, questions about sexual differences, and overt curiosity about exactly where babies come from.[67]

The American Academy of Pediatrics has indicated that sexual behavior problems in young children include any act that:

- Occurs frequently and can't be redirected

- Causes emotional or physical pain or injury to themselves or others, such as inserting objects in body openings

- Is associated with physical aggression or involves coercion or force

- Simulates adult sexual acts[68]

Most parents are notoriously bad at talking with their children about sex and sexuality. Many avoid the subject entirely and just let their kids learn what it's all about from peers or other sources. However, because of all the misinformation that's out there and potential risks involved, a parent's very basic responsibility relative to children's sexuality includes the following:

- Using appropriate language for body parts (ex. calling a penis "penis," not your "wee-wee,") and teaching children which parts are private (those covered by a swimsuit).

- Evaluating and encouraging the family's respect for modesty.

- Reinforcing the idea that their body is their own, and they have the right to protect it.

- Explaining what good and bad touch are (e.g., bad touch is the kind they don't like or feel good about and want to stop right away); making sure they understand that if anyone tries to touch them in a bad way, they should tell you right away; sharing with them a rule that it is NOT okay for anyone to look at or touch their private parts.

- Controlling exposure to sexually explicit material, including that on the media.

- Answering questions about sexuality honestly and in a matter-of-fact way without laughing, reacting in anger, or shaming the child for being curious about such things; not going into more detail than necessary or getting long-winded about a question; always finishing with, "Did that answer your question?"[69]

The acronym LGBTQ stands for Lesbian, Gay, Bi-sexual, Transsexual and Queer (not exclusively heterosexual) or Questioning (still unsure about one's sexual orientation). Some children may experience confusion and difficulty in fusing their gender-role identification (behaviors, abilities, and characteristics associated with a particular gender) with their sex at birth. Eventually, they may claim they are transsexual. Others who develop and continue to have sexual feelings for individuals of the same gender will come to understand that they are bi-sexual, lesbian, or gay and identify as homosexual rather than heterosexual.

Parents who question the science surrounding LGBTQ beginnings and see certain behavior as aberrant or against their religious views are not likely be supportive if their child manifests what parents see as atypical sexual behavior. They worry about the child's future, worry about what their friends and relatives will think, and worry about what their relationship with the child will be like if they reject the child or if they accept the "condition." Some may think they've done something wrong to make their child "that way" and feel guilty, not understanding that homosexuality is not something that is contagious or learned. They may be advised by someone that there are cures for "this sort of thing." That kind of ill-informed thinking and advice can set up all kinds of problems.

Parents who become aware of a child's atypical sexual preference and are unaccepting of it will benefit from learning as much as possible about homosexuality and gender identification from a factual and unbiased source. That could be a *knowledgeable* physician or therapist, an LGBTQ support group, or evidence-based and scientifically accurate literature dealing with healthy sexuality.[70,71] This would serve to open up the sort of communication that will be needed between family members if they are to continue to respect and support one another, care for one another, and remain intact.

Cultural and Ethnic Diversity

Just as psychosexual identity and behavior is age-related, so is our awareness and understanding of ethnicity and people from diverse cultures. While people differ culturally, anthropologists believe that all contemporary societies share certain commonalities such as ways for groups to establish criteria for who can be a member in a particular group and who can't. Societies pass on that cultural knowledge to their children, and there are consequences for transgressing the rules related to those cultural values. That doesn't mean that things can't change or that culture is fixed. It actually does change over time in the process of people observing and interacting with others and living their own lives. In other words, culture is always a work in progress.[72] It may be that factors such as the media, music, and travel today are speeding up certain changes.

As early as two years of age, children are already becoming aware of others' physical characteristics and cultural behaviors that are different from their own. Some are initially frightened of people who are very different in appearance. I remember when working in Beijing, China, and taking a day to walk a portion of the Great Wall. As I came up through one of the parapets, a Chinese child about 18 months of age stared at me and then burst out crying. Her parents were embarrassed, smiled at me apologetically, and then explained in Chinese to the tour guide that the child was from a rural area and had never before seen a white person. Later, the tour guide explained to me that white people are sometimes referred to in China as "ghosts."

By 4 and 5, children begin to classify others on the basis of gender, color, age, family structures, socioeconomic class, and other aspects. This is the beginning of "us" and "them" with respect to race and ethnicity, and human beings are biologically programmed to notice general differences among Black, White, Asian, and

Hispanic or Latino playmates in terms of skin color, eye color and shape, hair texture, shape of lips and other facial characteristics.[73] As a rejection stage builds, they begin to choose friends that are similar in gender and race. They may begin to develop stereotypes about others, particularly if they hear them modeled within their family, extended family, or peer group.

By 6, some children are already discriminating against others based on identity, teasing others who are different, and rejecting some who don't share their race, ethnicity, or lifestyle. Ideas about being in an "in-group" with others who are similar and "out-groups" consisting of everyone else who is different racially, ethnically, and culturally appears by about 7 and 8 years of age when children may begin to experience bias and conflict with others based on these differences.[74] That's the time when you will want to be on the lookout for confusion, misconceptions, or negativity related to your child's perspectives about diversity if you want to raise a child with as few biases and prejudicial attitudes as possible.

You will also want to be sensitive to any concern from your own children about tensions or conflicts they're experiencing with others that are meant to be demeaning, discriminatory, or threatening. Their developing self-concept is heavily influenced by verbal assaults and other behaviors directed at making them feel ashamed of their appearance, social status, race, ethnicity, and sexuality. Discuss why it's necessary to have the courage to speak up and to get beyond worrying about offending someone when it's clear the other person(s) meant to be offensive. Make sure that if your children ever feel they can't handle a situation or feel unsafe, they know they should find an adult to help.

Children benefit from opportunities to become personally acquainted with children and families from other ethnic and cultural groups, as well as from the many children's books, videos, and films about diversity. You can find annotated lists of these on the internet. Taking part in ethnic community festivals and learning about individual and cultural differences in people from other countries via the internet and travel are also ways to broaden children's positive perspectives about diversity.

If we want our children to develop values that include social justice and healthy attitudes toward others who differ from them, we have to avoid such pitfalls as being overprotective, ignoring faulty information and slurs about those in diverse populations, and inadvertently using stereotypical and demeaning language ourselves. If you hear your children make demeaning jokes or stereotypical remarks ("That guy's a homo." "Jeremy's dad is a nurse. I thought only girls could be nurses!" "We always sit Indian style in reading class." "Grandpa says he Jewed him down."), have a conversation with them. Sometimes, they don't realize the meaning of what they're saying. In a calm, matter-of-fact, and firm tone, let them know that the joke, word, phrase, or unkind reference you heard is unacceptable to you and why it is—that unfair treatment of others leads to the kinds of individual hurt and social unrest we've been experiencing in our country. As in other behaviors you don't want to see them repeat, be clear about consequences and follow through if you continue to hear negative slights and smears. Let them know that you want them to grow up treating all people with respect and fairness.

Extreme Shyness and Social Anxiety Disorder (SAD)

When I was thinking about significant differences in children, I couldn't leave out the 9-12% of children who are excessively shy when they're little, don't seem to be able to grow out of it, and have to endure the ongoing pain of it. In its most extreme form, it's diagnosed as Social Anxiety Disorder or SAD. A formal diagnosis would include the following criteria:[75]

- Unreasonable fear in social situations, disproportionate to the actual event

- Exposure to the feared situation causes significant levels of anxiety, distress, or avoidance

- The anxiety, distress, or avoidance results in a significant disruption of daily life functioning

- The fear, anxiety, or avoidance must have a duration of more than 6 months

- The fear, anxiety, or avoidance cannot be caused by a substance abuse or a secondary condition (i.e., stuttering) unless the reaction is significantly more than typical given the situation

Parents of socially anxious children worry that their child is going to experience a lonely existence as an adult, have trouble getting somewhere in the world of work, and continue to suffer from their extreme self-consciousness. Unfortunately, that can happen. Unless treatment is successful, persistent and intense fear of being negatively scrutinized by others can exist across a lifetime.[76] Social anxiety can interfere with normal development, severely limit potential and performance, and cripple a child's ability to make friends. In true situations with SAD, the anxiety that children experience is a combination of *physical symptoms* (feeling light-headed, nausea, shaky hands, headaches, heart palpitations, sense of panic), *cognitive beliefs* (others are judging me in a negative way; I'm so socially awkward; I'm going to fail), and *behavioral actions* (avoiding social situations or speaking up; mumbling; shaking, nail biting).[77]

That's a lot to live with on a daily basis, and children with social anxiety cope in a variety of ways that can make the situation worse. They may do this by refusing to go to school, avoiding asking others for help, selective mutism, worrying for days or weeks before having to give an oral presentation, and skipping social events such as parties. Others steer clear of any effort to make new friends, becoming oppositional, or developing speech and language impairment disorders such as stuttering and other communication deficits. Some turn to the internet to connect with others who are also isolated in real life.

Researchers are looking at the physiological factors that seem to predispose a child to developing the disorder, such as brain chemistry involving dopamine utilization (also seen in introverted personalities), brain activation in the amygdala and prefrontal cortex of the brain, and inherited temperament.

Parenting styles can exacerbate the condition in children. Those who are overly concerned about what other people think of them and their children, are overinvolved in their children's lives ("helicopter" and "tiger" parents), and who tend to isolate their family from anything outside the immediate family structure tend to produce anxious children. They do this by wanting to protect their children from all sorts of imagined dangers, instilling in them that social connections are less valuable than high achievement and perfectionism, and interfering with the development of resilience.[78]

What's important is that parents are usually the first to recognize some of the symptoms that go along with children's early social anxiety and social withdrawal. Working with private counselors to see if their parenting style is contributing to the problem can be the first line of attack in terms of positive intervention. Parents must also enlist the help of those at school so that children can get help with social skills and behavior modification training, development of prosocial behavior and friendship building, and other layers of support they need to function.

It helps if parents can teach their children to be transparent about their anxiety, in other words, to own it, accept it, and move forward as much as possible. Keeping a journal and positive self-talk can help ("I can do this even if it's hard." "Stay calm. What's the worst that can happen?" "I've been through this before, and the worst I thought would happen didn't. It won't this time, either!"). Working on one skill at a time, such as recognizing and changing negative thoughts, is helpful. More than anything, a child with social anxiety needs to be able to relax at home in a supportive family environment where there are strong, caring relationships, clear roles and boundaries, fair consequences when rules are broken, and opportunities to make decisions and contribute to the well-being of one another.[79] That's the sort of safe haven we all need at home.

Psychologist Christine Fonseca[80] has said that while social anxiety is pervasive and difficult, it is not hopeless. That kind of thinking needs to be communicated to every child who is struggling with the overwhelming insecurity that comes along with social anxiety.

Giftedness

How smart are you, and in what ways are you smart? What do you know or believe about your children's intellectual abilities? Have you wondered if they're gifted?

There are all kinds of ways to look at human intelligence or how we acquire and apply knowledge and skills. Some see it as a unitary trait we're born with, an amount of something that can be timed, measured, and given a score. Using this method, about 68.26% of the population scores between 85-115 on an I.Q. test such as the Stanford Binet Intelligence Scale. Another 13.59% fall between 115-130. Only 2.14% score between 130-145 and just 13 out of 10,000 or .13 fall between 145-160. Only 1 out of 30,000 score above that, and even fewer score above 180.

Some school systems still use this kind of testing as their primary method to determine who's gifted and who's not, selecting only those who score above 130 as potentially gifted. Unfortunately, such an outmoded concept as a score on a standardized IQ or achievement test doesn't tell us much more about the test taker other than that his or her score ranged somewhere from below average to very bright. A score could also mean that a child was sick that day, tired, anxious, or disinterested in taking the test.

Recent thinking about giftedness makes it clear that while intelligence is definitely an integral part of giftedness, it is not the same thing, nor is intelligence enough by itself to engender giftedness. Joseph Renzulli, a pioneer in gifted education, considered what he called a three-ring conception of giftedness (see Fig. 4.1) that included: 1) above average intellectual ability; 2) creativity, and 3) task commitment. Only if those three elements are working together, he said, can it result in high achievement or gifted behavior, and it would only "occur in certain people at certain times and in certain circumstances."[81] Researchers agree that it is less likely to happen in traditional academic environments where *deductive learning* directed at arriving at the right answer predominates. Rather, it is more apt to occur in *inductive educational environments* where children are encouraged to seek new information from engaging, interdisciplinary work, are able to experiment, and are assisted in analyzing and reporting what they find. Some parents have done that themselves by providing a place, equipment, and materials in their home for their children to "mess around" with their interests. Said one gifted adult about his childhood and parents, "They allowed anything short of burning down the house."

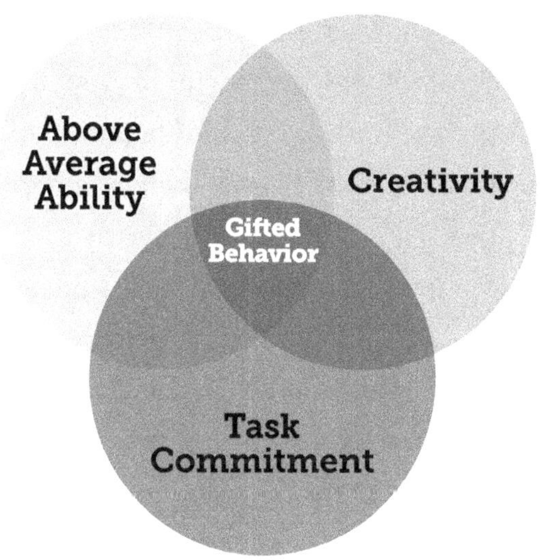

Fig. 4.1: 3-Ring Venn diagram of Renzulli's model[82]

Another way to look at the relationship of intelligence to giftedness is to think about the fact that human beings are intelligent in different ways. Howard Gardner, Harvard University psychologist sees intelligence as the ability to solve a problem or make something that is valued by a culture. He believes that human beings exhibit giftedness or extraordinary problem solving within a set of varied, inherited skills: verbal-linguistic, logical-mathematical, musical-rhythmic, bodily kinesthetic, visual-spatial, interpersonal, intrapersonal, and environmentalist-naturalist.[83,84] He and other academics concede there could be more, such as existential or digital aptitudes.

Giftedness, they say, is more complex than the mere capacity for storing, retrieving, and processing information. That makes sense relative to what can be observed in superb athletes who perform at remarkable levels (think LeBron James and Mickey Mantle); the genius in artists such as Leonardo DaVinci, Prince, Jimi Hendrix, Pablo Picasso and Mozart; physicists Elon Musk, Einstein, Marie Curie, and Stephen Hawking; the keen acumen of businesspeople like Warren Buffet, Oprah Winfrey, Ingvar Kamprad, Bill Gates, and Jeff Bezos; authors Franz Kafka, Anton Chekhov, and Ernest Hemingway; and the minds of chess masters like Garry Kasparov and Judit Polgar. There isn't room here to list people in every diverse category who are clearly so much more analytical, creative, clever, and insightful than almost all other human beings. They are our inventors, athletes, writers, artists, problem solvers, entertainers, and history makers. Those who are critical of what Gardner has labeled "multiple intelligences or frames of mind" see these as *talents,* not necessarily markers of intellectual ability and note that they range from virtually absent in some people to virtually superior in others.

Another popular concept of intelligence that fits well with giftedness is that of Robert Sternberg with his triarchic theory[85] that we mentally manage our lives in primarily analytical, creative, or practical ways. In other words, we may be able to function or survive without a particular skill or talent, but we cannot survive without being able to adjust to and manage the world around us in terms of our own ability. People do this in different ways, capitalizing on their strengths and making up for their weaknesses. Also, a person may be very adept at solving abstract problems but not very creative or astute at solving everyday problems in the real world.[86] Conversely, we see the opposite in street children such as those in the Philippines or Brazil who survive without the support of any adults and through sheer "street smarts."

In terms of whether or not children are truly gifted, rather than advanced because of rich experiences and a supportive family, psychologists and neurologists agree that the brains of gifted children *are* different. There is evidence that children with truly special cognitive abilities and talents are not just at the extreme higher end of normal distribution on intelligence tests but think and behave in unique ways. They function in an accelerated manner, and gifted children may be especially talented in one area (ex. music, art, mathematics, literacy) but not in other areas. They think about their specialized area in unusual ways, ask questions about it, and are eager to "get at it." Guidelines that are useful in assessing whether or not children are truly gifted include the following:[87]

- Seek constant mental stimulus and have a need to explore those subjects in which they're interested in extraordinary depth

- Have insatiable curiosity; constant questioning and inquiry

- Demonstrate precision in thinking and expression

- Have advanced vocabulary, language, reading, and/or math skills

- Display an acquired extensive general knowledge about the world

- Show an ability to learn more quickly, easily, and independently than peers

- Exhibit advanced and efficient cognitive processes and learning strategies; ability to learn and process complex information rapidly

- Show considerable flexibility in ideas and approaches to tasks

- Have high standards for performance (sometimes to the point of unhealthy perfectionism)

- Demonstrate high motivation to accomplish challenging tasks; boredom during easy or repetitious tasks

- Display positive self-concept, especially with regard to academic endeavors

It's important to point out that precocious children are not without their specialized problems. Some of the world's most talented individuals, including Albert Einstein, Thomas Edison, Lewis Carroll, Winston Churchill, Jay Leno, Whoopi Goldberg, and Tom Cruise were thought to be seriously learning disabled in their early years. None of their strong interests and needs as children were recognized, and many of them and others like them struggled because of one or more of the following:[88]

- Asynchronous development—being very different from their age mates and preferring to interact with adults rather than peers; may turn peers off because of solitary interest in advanced ideas, use of advanced vocabulary

- Poor ability to read social cues, resulting in being seen as odd or weird by others; bullied; inability to work well on group projects

- Inadequate testing, identification, and evaluation; faulty conceptions of giftedness by their parents or an educational system that equated giftedness and talent with conformity, rapid learning, and early maturation.

- Focus by adults primarily on cognitive areas of development and less attention to child's affective or prosocial development

- Co-existence of disabilities such as ADHD, autism, learning difficulties

- Boredom and resulting behavioral problems.

- Frustration or intolerance with others who don't think as quickly

- Intentionally hiding abilities in order to fit in with peers

- Disorganization; carelessness in work and daily living habits

- Poor social skills: poor listener; argumentative, disrespectful, uncooperative and not interested in others' opinions; disruptive; dominates discussions; acts like a "know-it-all"

- Unrealistic expectations by adults that if a child excels in one area, they should be able to excel in all academic areas

- Teachers who don't know what to do with them and simply pile on more work and worksheets; traditional, restrictive academic systems with respect to gifted education.

Giftedness is always intertwined and connected with finding and solving the problems that emerge in cultures over time. In that way, Howard Gardner believes that because our children today live in a world of relentless change and a constant outpouring of new information, parents and teachers can contribute to all children's developing problem solving abilities and potential by shaping what he describes as "Five Minds for the Future":[89]

- **A disciplined mind**—one that learns at least one profession as well as the major thinking (science, math, history, etc.) behind it

- **A synthesizing mind**—one that is able to organize massive amounts of information and communicate it effectively to others

- **A creative mind**—one that revels in unasked questions and uncovering new phenomena

- **A respectful mind**—one that appreciates the differences between human beings and can understand and work with all persons

- **An ethical mind**—one that is moved to fulfill responsibility as a worker and as a citizen[90]

Children with Special Needs

Amazingly, only in about 5 percent of the time will children be born with defects that result in disabilities. However, despite efforts to prevent prenatal threats to development, studies indicate that 10-20 percent of women across all socioeconomic and racial categories continue to use psychoactive chemicals, alcohol, or tobacco during pregnancy, possibly contributing to adverse physical and/or neurological alterations in a fetus. Other defects can be the result of genetic disorders, missing or extra chromosomes, and environmental factors that include infectious diseases.[91] The resulting challenges range from mild to severe. Some can be corrected or modified, and some will be life-long lasting. Parents vary in their coping abilities, the decisions they have to make about their child's education and care, and the types and amounts of support they have. Consider these parents in a community panel on handicapping conditions in families:

Bonnie talked about her daughter's mental retardation. "She seemed perfect when she was born, and she still looks perfect. From the outside you could never tell anything is wrong, but we realized by the time she was 2 that there were going to be pretty severe problems intellectually and emotionally. I remember that when she was 6 or 7, she would frequently throw awful tantrums in a store when she didn't get what she wanted. I would hustle her out to the car, and she'd be kicking and screaming and trying to hit me. People would always look at us as if I was a terrible, abusive mother with an out-of-control kid, not understanding that she couldn't help how she was behaving and that I was doing the best I could under the circumstances. You can tell when a child has something like cerebral palsy or another physical malady, but things like autism and mental retardation are more hidden.

They're harder to deal with in public.

Peg shared that her focus on caring for a daughter's cerebral palsy had cost her marriage. "She just needed so much care that there wasn't any room for anything or anybody else. After my husband left, I remember blaming her for that and being so angry with her. One time, I was brushing her hair, and she kept saying "Oww, owww" because I was brushing too hard. And the more she twisted and tried to get me to stop, the harder I brushed. After she got on the van to go to the center she was attending, I just sat down and cried. I was so ashamed—and also scared that things were so out of control. I got on the phone with the therapist I had been seeing and told him that I was done. I couldn't handle it anymore. Thankfully, she's still home with me but I had to learn what to do *before* things become overwhelming—because, at times, they still do.

A father on the panel spoke about the devastation he and his wife felt when their son was born with Down Syndrome. They knew instantly because of his characteristic facial appearance, and their doctor confirmed it, based on a number of other physical features and chromosomal analysis that he had indeed inherited 3 copies of chromosome 21 instead of the usual 2. "So, we expected the worst. Turns out that he does have some of the problems associated with the disorder, a thing with his heart, some motor issues, and hearing loss. But other than that, he's now 8 and pretty much like any other kid. We were told when he was born that all kids with Down Syndrome are happy-go-lucky and extra loving, but that's just a myth. Like our other two kids, he has his share of cranky and uncooperative days, as well as happy and affectionate times. My wife and I got over all that stuff we were feeling when he was first born, and we feel lucky to have him in our lives. In fact, we can't imagine being without him and hope he feels the same way."

Eric joined in, adding information about a nephew who's been diagnosed with Asperger's Syndrome. "Everyone just thought the kid was antisocial. He is definitely book smart but right from the time he was in second grade, they started having problems with him in school. He'd just blurt out silly things in class. He's 11 now, and the main thing is that he just doesn't have any friends. Kids make fun of him at school, and my sister and brother-in-law have had a hell of a time getting him out of bed in the morning to go to school. I guess it's like a milder form of autism. They've tried to get him involved in sports, but he's so uncoordinated that they've given that up. He's an absolute wizard on the computer, so I guess he's got a future there."

Susan spoke to the group about a problem that developed in her family because of their unrealistic expectations of their two sons, one of them born with a number of birth defects. "When our twin boys were born, David had absolutely nothing wrong, and Robby had so many issues that it's a wonder he made it at all. Despite Robby's health issues, the boys were fairly close until they started school. That's when David started developing new friends and wanted to spend time with them. He didn't want Robby always tagging along, but we insisted that he include his brother. My husband and I both thought that David was being unfair, that if he didn't want to include his brother in his play with others, he could just stay home or not invite anyone over. That was our first big mistake. We also told David more than once how lucky he was to be so healthy and that he could have been the one who ended up with problems, hoping that he'd feel guilty enough to keep including Robby. Of course, what happened was that David really began to resent his brother and what had initially been a really loving relationship between the two of them just fell apart. I guess everyone in our family but us realized what was happening. It was my mother-in-law's honest concerns and comments about what we were doing that brought us to our senses. I know that took a lot of courage on her part. We backed off on our demands and, eventually, things went back to being more normal. Because we weren't insisting that David always include Robby, he was more willing to do so, especially with one little boy they both really enjoy playing with.

Other parents and those in the audience talked about additional disabling conditions or had questions about common disabilities, such as attention-deficit/hyperactivity disorder (ADHD), Autism Spectrum Disorder, and sensory processing problems. Some spoke about how hard it was to handle orthopedic impairment, severe visual and hearing deficiencies, and chronic illnesses. They shared their concerns about the lack of social acceptance by other children, unwanted curiosity and rude comments by unfamiliar people, and negative attitudes by parents of "normal" children who believed that placing children with disabilities in their child's classroom took too much of the teacher's time and attention away from the class in general. Some spoke of 24/7 responsibility in taking care of children with disabilities and how hard it was to find respite from the constant, overwhelming obligations, financial issues, and concerns about their child's future. Those who had fully dependent children admitted that they were apprehensive about who would take care of their child when they were no longer able to.

Clearly, parents of children with exceptional needs face additional pressures. Sometimes, what helps is just having someone who listens or someone who can provide a bit of respite care occasionally. Other parents obviously need better connections with a formal intervention system for information and guidance about assessment, health matters, referrals, educational placement, financial assistance, and family member issues. They may benefit from working with professionals to help with depression, reevaluate long-term expectations, redefine parental roles, and identify strategies to improve parenting competencies.[92] For children with less severe disabilities, programs that offer individual training in independence and prosocial skill building can go a long way in helping them feel more included with peers, more resilient, and better able to make gains in developmental achievement.

Questions Parents Ask

Q: Ever since he's been little, our son has liked to dress up and play with dolls. Now that he's older, he's not doing that as much, but he's very effeminate. At school, he'd rather hang around with the girls than the boys and some of them have started calling him Mary. His name is Martin. The worst thing is—he says he doesn't mind it when they call him a girl's name, that he likes it. He's only 7, so do you think he'll grow out of all this? How early can you tell if someone's gay or not? My husband is really uptight about it.

A: Other than child sexual abuse, children's sexuality is a neglected science. First of all, it's a private thing, and parents don't even like to think their children have sexual feelings, let alone have a researcher talk to them about it. Also, children are harder to study because they don't understand much about their own sexuality and don't have the verbal skills to describe aspects of it. We do know this: Not all little boys who like to play with dolls or dress up grow up to be gay; nor do all little girls who like to rough house and play tee ball turn out to be lesbians.[93] Some do become what is called gender non-conforming, and some don't. Current research by neuroscientists, endocrinologists, geneticists, and cognitive psychologists is yielding some answers about how heterosexuality or homosexuality is determined, particularly studies of fetal brain development and differences in emergent hypothalamic structures. They are different in those who become gay or lesbian and, while homosexuality is found in significantly fewer people in the population, it's important to understand that it is not abnormal, nor is it a chosen lifestyle. There is growing evidence that biological and genetic factors play a determining part. Being gay, lesbian, straight, bisexual, or transsexual results from differences in genes and sex hormones in interaction with the developing brain.[94] Adults who have been studied report that they knew very early that they were sexually attracted to peers of the same gender. Many had to endure shame, guilt, derision, or bullying while growing up, simply because of a difference as inherent as one's green eyes or height.

It is critical that parents examine their attitudes about homosexuality. To see it as some sort of disappointing imperfection in a child or something the child can and should "correct" is cruel and harmful. Ultimately, that perspective is detrimental to the parent-child relationship, injurious to a child's self-worth, and can lead to significant mental health issues. Perhaps we're making progress in according the acceptance and respect all LGBTQ children and adults deserve when we see how many Americans supported Pete Buttigieg, a Rhodes scholar, Afghanistan war veteran, mayor of South Bend, Indiana, and gay man in his candidacy for President of the United States. Obviously, his sexuality was deemed no more important than his intelligence, courage, social aptitude, communication acumen, or leadership abilities. He has often spoken about the unconditional support and love his parents provided for him while he was growing up and later as an "outed" adult. Maybe that made everything else possible.

Q: Our daughter Kelsey is one of only two Black children in her 3rd grade class in a school-of-choice program. The teacher is White, as are all the other children. We chose to have Kelsey attend it because the curriculum is based on STEM (Science, Technology, Engineering and Math). My husband is an industrial engineer, and we both want our daughter to benefit from that kind of content and creative thinking. She loves the program but has told us that whenever the kids are paired up together for a project, the teacher asks her to work with the other Black child, never with a White child. We don't want to raise any hackles with the teacher, but we feel like we need to say something. Should we?

A: Absolutely. It could be that the teacher is either unaware that she's setting apart the two children based on their ethnicity or she feels she's doing them a favor by "allowing" them to always work together. Without understanding the situation, she's unintentionally teaching more than STEM. She's instilling that segregation is a good thing, that White belongs with White and Black belongs only with Black. Best practice would call for her to focus not only on academic content but to take advantage of the classroom diversity to expand children's understanding of and respect for one another as they share their ideas, opinions, and values with one another.

Respectfully, ask if the children might be allowed to choose their partners or small groups for the next project instead of working with a designated partner. Talk with your daughter about who she'd choose among her classmates for a partner and why. Be sure you're offering opportunities for your daughter to have multi-ethnic playdates and experiences outside of school. Also, if your husband has time, it would be beneficial for him to design an age-appropriate STEM project for all the children and work with the teacher to implement it, demonstrating the ethnic diversity and collaboration they are all sure to experience later in the workplace.

Q: Our son is autistic, and his behavior at school is horrendous. He has a shadow teacher who sticks fairly close to him, along with the regular classroom teacher. Still, no one seems to be able to control him. He strikes out at classmates without warning if he thinks they're "not being nice to him." Most of the kids avoid him except for one little girl who sort of "mothers" him. Both teachers are nice, but I'm not sure how much learning or behavior modification is going on in that he just seems to wander the room most of the time, doing nothing. As long as he doesn't get into trouble with another child, they just allow him to do whatever he wants. Even at group time when all the other children are listening to a story, he rarely joins the circle or is even asked to. He plays continually with a Lego set they have but never builds anything and just lines them up. How can I know if he's in the right type of educational environment? He's 5 1/2, by the way.

A: Children with any kind of PPD (Pervasive Developmental Disorder) can be a significant challenge to both parents and teachers, particularly with language delay and disruptive or aggressive behavior. I'm assuming you've had him tested thoroughly to assess his social reciprocity, communication ability, restricted patterns of behavior, and any other disabilities or disorders he might have. I'm also assuming that your development team outlined a comprehensive treatment plan for the following: 1) fostering development; 2) promoting learning; 3) reducing rigidity and stereotypy; 4) eliminating maladaptive behaviors, and 5) alleviating family distress.[95] It sounds as if you're not sure the first four are happening on his behalf. It's important for his future functioning that pragmatic language and social skills are being developed as much as possible.

Meet with his classroom and shadow teachers together to talk about your concerns and to see how accurate they are. Respectfully ask how each is working with him to build his strengths in communication, social interactions, and self-care. Ask them for specifics.

Currently, there is controversy about the best placement for very young children with autistic disorder. Should it be inclusion in the least restrictive environment as with your son or should it be in a specialized educational setting where teachers have special training and experience in providing focused support for a particular disorder? Obviously, there can be advantages and drawbacks to both. After meeting with his classroom teachers to make sure they are making an earnest effort to address his needs and having at least some success, decide whether or not you need to arrange a meeting with his development team to see if any changes need to be made in his educational plan and program or if he needs a change in setting and personnel. You're the best advocate your son can have.

Q: We just moved here from Atlanta. Neighborhood kids play in the park across the street and have even come to the door and asked our daughter to join them a couple of times. When she sees them approaching the house, she hides in her bedroom until they're gone. Her teacher says she's the same way at school and that she sits by herself in the lunchroom and finds something to do by herself on the playground at recess. I was a little shy when I was a kid but nothing like this! She was this way in her last school, and we'd like to have her make a better start here. How do we do that?

A: First, it would be important to determine whether your daughter is extremely shy or actually suffering from Social Anxiety Disorder (SAD). Both can produce anxiety, but the feelings that result from SAD are much more intense and potentially debilitating. It's likely that she's struggling every day, worrying about how she's perceived by her new teacher and classmates. The move adds unfamiliar factors and challenges. She's experiencing a lot of newness: home, school, neighbors, classmates, and teachers. Outgoing kids would welcome all of this because it brings more attention and the excitement of new friends, but the SAD child feels overwhelmed, may experience panic attacks, and feel completely out of control. Be sensitive to what she needs right now and the fact that she may be exhausted from trying to cope and constantly anticipating the worst happening at school. Tell her that you know how hard it is to ask for help in school when she needs it, but how important that is. Talk about some strategies for responding to invitations or questions from peers and suggest some scripts. Provide opportunities to talk with her about what goes on at school. When there are negative thoughts or self-talk ("Kids just don't like me. They think I'm weird."), talk about the importance of converting them. Suggest that she tell herself right away to stop and replace the thought with a positive one ("I'm okay. It's going to be okay."), that she actually has the power to do that. Share the issue with her teachers so they can help reduce her fear of being the center of attention and provide support in building friendships with other children. It would help greatly to get a formal diagnosis with a competent therapist who can also provide her with ideas for handling her emotions and ways to build social competency and communication skills.

Q: This is something we don't understand very well. Our son has had a serious issue with learning to read in first grade this year, and his spelling is atrocious. His teacher says he should be tested for a reading disability. Yet, we have been told that he qualifies for the school's gifted program beginning in grade 2. Will he outgrow his reading issues?

A: The short answer is that your son could outgrow these issues if they're only developmental in nature. If they aren't, it will be important to understand the neurological differences he's experiencing and to arm him with effective strategies to deal with them. It's not uncommon for gifted children to have some kind of accompanying learning disability—a difference in brain organization. Such children are designated in school systems as "twice exceptional or 2e." They are unique in that they have the characteristics of gifted children; yet they may struggle with dyslexia, dysgraphia, dyscalculia, or other disabilities.[96] It may or may not be a learning disability as the teacher is suggesting, but it's good that she's at least considering it. Cognitive issues in young children and especially in boys can be due to asynchronous development and cognitive discrepancies.[97] It wouldn't be surprising to find that his handwriting and spelling are still a little "iffy" due to normal developmental issues that could disappear in a year or two. Twice exceptional development gets easier to diagnose by the time a child is 7 and 8, but gifted children are particularly at risk. Some are able to hide or make up for phonological awareness weaknesses because they have such good verbal short term memory and knowledge of grammar and vocabulary.[98] Also, teachers or parents may not believe they need special services because they appear bright and might assign their difficulties to not paying attention or not working hard enough. A couple of questions: Do you have a relative with dyslexia? Is your son still having trouble identifying left and right, creating rhyming words, remembering sight words, breaking words into syllables, or sounding out unknown words by stretching sounds together? These can be clues that would suggest the need for formal assessment and possible dyslexia. While we want to be patient, it's also true that early intervention is important so that skills training can be provided to ward off developing a pattern of academic failure.

Red Flags

1. Overreacting to children's normal or divergent sexual behavior or failing to intervene when their behavior is clearly not appropriate.

2. Ignoring questions children have about sexuality or promoting myths (ex. "The stork brings babies." "Masturbation causes blindncss.").

3. Rejection or demeaning of children because of atypical sexual preferences (ex. "masculine" dress preferences in girls or boys who prefer playing with dolls and dress-up clothes).

4. Family members making stereotypical remarks, jokes, references or negative slurs related to another person's gender identity, sexuality or ethnicity.

5. Parents feeling angry, helpless, depressed, exhausted, or overwhelmed; Ignoring their own needs when caring for a child with special needs; refusal to admit the need for respite or where to find it.

6. Social anxiety that is expressed in fear, anxiety, and avoidance to the extent that it results in a child's problematic daily functioning.

7. Focusing only on a child's physical and cognitive progress and ignoring affective or interpersonal development.

8. Equating giftedness only with intelligence and not taking into consideration the need for creativity and task commitment.

9. Expecting a gifted child to be precocious and talented in all areas of development.

10. The use of psychoactive chemicals, alcohol, or tobacco during pregnancy.

What's in Your Parenting Toolkit?

1. Avoid any tendency to overprotect children so they can develop as much autonomy as possible.

2. Work closely with a child's teacher and other professionals to communicate concerns, areas of frustration, child's interests, and to share with one another adaptive strategies that work to address any behavioral matters.

3. Use picture books, videos, films, the internet, friendships, and travel to broaden children's acquaintance with other ethnicities and cultures.

4. Reinforce children's understanding of good and bad touch.

5. Enlist the help of other professionals for a child's social anxiety.

6. Make sure a gifted child has access to inductive, engaging, and challenging academic settings.

7. Access special skills training for children who are socially awkward or having trouble making friends.

8. Make full use of formal intervention systems to evaluate, plan for, and support a child with a disabling condition.

9. Model respect for differences in people; address stereotypical language or remarks directly and in a nonjudgmental manner.

Conclusion

By the time we are adults, our positive or biased beliefs about differences we see in others have become fairly ingrained. Since our natural tendency is to raise our children with the same values we have, we need to be very intentional about examining those perspectives to make sure they will serve our children well for their current and future interactions with others. We can give them a gift, or we can give them an incumbrance. In a world that demands more than ever active prejudice prevention and reduction, we have the awesome responsibility to rigorously teach and model fair-mindedness and empathy toward others and to reinforce our children's motivation to treat others with caring and respect.

CHAPTER 5

What Happens If There's A Divorce?

Phil: "Tommie and I have been divorced for 3 years now, but we still take being parenting Alexander very seriously. Maybe people think we're screwy or just trying to "hang on to each other," but we want to parent him together. We talk about him often, go to his school events together, and keep his best interests in mind when we make decisions about him. Thankfully, our new partners are okay with this and don't feel threatened. In fact, we all feel that he just has more people who care about him. We're good…"

Joe DiMaggio, Jr.: "My father was totally missing from my childhood…. We were on the cover of the first Sport magazine when it came out in 1949, my father and I, me wearing a little No. 5 jersey. I was taken to the photo session (and) we had the picture taken. My father and I didn't say two words. When I decided to leave college and join the Marines, I called my father to tell him…. and he said, 'The Marines are a good thing,' and there was nothing more for us to say to each other." [99]

Couples aren't thinking about divorce when they decide to spend the rest of their lives together. It's just not in the plan. Nevertheless, almost half of first marriages still currently end in divorce, causing more than 1 million children a year in the U.S. to experience a family shakeup and breakup.

Family stress may go on for long periods of time before one or both parents finally make the decision to end their marriage. When asked what the most painful experience in their lives has been, most people describe the death of a loved one or the end of a marriage or relationship. Divorces are accompanied by all the problems associated with relationships that have become messy, the fractured ties that often go along with divorce, and the time it takes to regain a new footing. This chapter has been included for those of you who are considering or have experienced this reality.

Effects on Children

If the road to separation and divorce has been a long one for you and your partner, you might think that your children will be just as relieved to see the end of a bad marriage as you are. That's a myth. Another modern fairytale is that because so many marriages today end in divorce, causing many of your children's friends to be in the same situation, it won't be all that traumatic for them. Not so. Children are unable to intellectualize divorce, and that is especially true when they are very young.

Most divorces occur when parents are between the ages of 25 and 39, many who have dependent children. At least half of these children will grow up with parents who continue to stay angry at one another. Three out of five of them will feel rejected by at least one of their parents. It doesn't have to be this way. Children can and do recover from divorce when they have parents who remain reliable, loving, caring, and supportive.

The effects of divorce vary with children's ages and depend

on the circumstances surrounding the divorce. While every child is different and may react in different ways to divorce, there are some common reactions by age group.[100]

Babies and Toddlers

Common Characteristics and Behaviors Seen

- Sensitive to changes in people they depend on for primary care because they haven't learned to understand the emotions they are feeling

- Confusion, anxiety, and fear

- Trouble sleeping

- Unwillingness to leave custodial parent; clingy behavior

- Excessive crankiness; frequent crying

- Somewhat slower in learning new skills.

What Parents Can Do

- Stay in their lives in a consistent and constant way. Know that *both* fathers and mothers are important in these early years and that parents play very different roles in building trust, self-esteem, and confidence. It's often assumed that children of this age are too young to notice one parent being gone, but that isn't true. All children need to develop an attachment to *both* of their parents, to be nurtured by both of them, to play with both of them (since fathers play in an entirely different way with their children), and to learn from both of them.

Preschoolers

Common Characteristics and Behaviors Seen

- Children 2-5 suffer the most severe short- and long-term effects when parents split up. They are highly susceptible to unstable daily routines and are dependent on both parents as a source of nurturance and help.

- They may feel a parent has left because they were naughty, resulting in intense guilt feelings.
- May feel abandoned and afraid they will have no place to live, may cry, whine, cling, become overly demanding, and have temper tantrums.
- May worry about what else can happen (Will the non-custodial parent take the dog? Will they be able to see their grandparents?).
- May return to security items (blanket, thumb…) to resolve their emotional neediness.
- May have lapses in toilet training; sleep problems may appear.
- May worry about the other parent leaving and become eager to please in order to avoid imagined abandonment.
- Play is negatively affected, especially creative play and art expression.
- May be regression (bed-wetting, soiling pants, prior eating problems reappearing).
- May refuse to play with other children or express inappropriate verbal or physical anger when playing
- May begin to prefer adult companionship.

What Parents Can Do

- Remain constant in the child's life and keep in control. Each parent provides a role model and contributes to the resolution of the Oedipus conflict (subconscious desire for parent of opposite sex), which is dealt with between three and six years of age when a boy should begin to identify more with his father and a girl with her mother.

- Be watchful for regression and be patient and supportive.

- Provide opportunities for monitored play with other children, since it functions as a way to express emotions, something they need for discharging the tension of the crisis they are experiencing.

- Respond to tantrums by ignoring them as much as possible or providing a "cooling down" place (not a corner or a chair) until the child can get back in control. Be careful not to give the child undue attention, since that will only prolong the tantrum and reinforce that kind of behavior. Stay calm (even though it's especially hard when you feel out of control and angry yourself); don't yell, lecture, moralize, shame, or be punitive to the child. They can't "hear" anything you have to say when they're out of control. Tell the child, "When you can stop screaming (kicking, crying, etc.), come back and join me, but not until then." Don't allow the child to hit or kick you and, once the child is back in control, change the subject. Don't praise the child for regaining control.

Elementary and Middle-School Aged Children
Common Characteristics and Behaviors Seen

- At this age, you may see profound sadness and a longing to have parents reunited and the child may work hard at it.

- There may be a lot of anger but no direct confrontation; instead, you may see it expressed in whining, physical complaints, fears, sleeplessness, and a significant drop in school achievement OR an *over-focus on* school achievement.

- Children may be caught in loyalty binds (Will my dad think I don't love him if I say I want to live with my mother? Why does my mom get so mad if I say I had a good time with my dad and stepmom on a visitation?).

What Parents Can Do

- Recognize that these children can feel as if their world is upside down; they feel very much out of control and anxious about what is going to happen for the future.

- Maintain structure, routine and limits. A predictable environment makes the child feel safe, secure, and loved.

- Don't assume your children know how much they mean to you.

- Hug them, touch them as you speak to them, looking them straight in the eye and saying, "I love you—a lot! That will never change."

- Be sensitive about the fact that their world includes greater peer involvement, homework, and extra-curricular activities. It may make their lives more complicated and difficult when they have to add long visitations to their schedule, much as they want to be with the non-custodial parent.

- Make sure that you receive and comment on their report cards; attend sports, extra-curricular events, and school activities.

- Do not blame the other parent or cut him or her down in front of the child. Since children's self-esteem is strongly linked to the image they have of each of their parents, you diminish your child's self-worth every time you speak of the other parent in negative terms.

- If you are the non-custodial parent, show up on time for all visitations.

What Your Children Need to Hear

We hope that you and your ex-spouse have taken time to sit down together with your children to explain the reasons for your divorce. You can be honest with them and try to explain it in terms they can understand. Before doing this, it's important that parents think very carefully about what children need to hear and what they *do not* need to hear. For example, they do *not* need to hear that one parent is "good" and the other parent is "bad." This is true, even if one of you feels that way about the other because of an affair, use of drugs, alcohol, or personality problems. Your children don't need to be burdened with details of what went wrong; they just need to know what will happen to *them.*

Some of the important things your children need to hear you say are:

- Though your marriage has ended, the family will continue, including relationships with the extended family on both sides. While adult feelings for one another can change, the special connection between parents and their children and the children's relationship with siblings, grandparents and other relatives goes on forever.

- You will continue taking care of them and providing for them.

- They had no part in the change of feelings between the adults. In no way did they cause that to change and, although they may wish they had the power to change the decision their parents have made, they *do not* have it.

- The decision you have made to divorce was not a whim, but a carefully thought out direction after a lot of effort went into trying to make the marriage work.

- You're sorry for the hurt this decision has caused for them.

- Although the divorce will bring changes in the amount of time spent with each parent, other areas and routines in their lives will continue—same school, house, friends, or whatever parents can manage that will remain the same.

- You understand that they will have a lot of concerns and certainly a lot of feelings about the divorce, and both of you will be available to listen.

The Importance of Consistency

During and after the divorce process, children need as much continuity, geographic stability, and predictability as their parents can provide. Being uprooted and moved away from their original family home causes multiple emotional, social, and activity losses, which compounds the loss of one parent for them. Do your best to maintain as much continuity as you can for your children. If at all possible, try to work things out so that your children stay in the family home, continue to go to the same school, and keep their same friends and routines. When children can maintain regular routines, they are less likely to be overwhelmed by the changes divorce brings.

Children need adequate financial support and care as they are growing up, and both parents need to contribute to this responsibly and fairly. When a non-custodial parent's attitude toward loss of custody remains one of intense disappointment or anger, or the parent was unstable or a poor parent to begin with, it becomes easier to dump all parenting responsibility into the lap of the custodial parent (You've got 'em—Now you take care of them!), including financial responsibility and total child care. The result can be severe stress overload in the custodial parent due to overwhelming economic and psychological responsibility and a marked decline in any leisure time. Opportunities to take on more responsibility at work or to return to school in order to prepare for work are often less possible. All of this can result in burnout in the custodial parent, not a good condition for rearing healthy children. The most unfortunate outcome is that children sense the other parent's lack of support, and the result is eventually a diminished respect for that parent.

Parents often get concerned after divorce when rules are different from home to home. Rules don't have to be the same in both households and usually are not. Children are pretty good adapters when they know what is expected of them. Just be very clear about the ground rules and restrictions in your home relative to chores, bedtimes, manners, and other issues. Try to get the other parent to be cooperative about discipline and major limitations (ex. homework has to be done; bedtime on a school night should be the same in both households; the child's commitment to extra-curricular responsibilities, such as Scout troop meetings and piano lessons, should be honored.)

Don't get into a discussion about the differences between your households with your children. Remember that they can play games, too. Simply let them know that they have certain boundaries in your home that may differ from the other parent's home. Tell them you expect them to follow through without challenging you about them.

Expect that if a child begins to feel that one parent is stricter than another and more apt to apply consequences when the child's behavior is out of line, the child may ask to go live with the more lenient parent. If guidance and discipline with the current custodial parent are not unreasonable or punitive, both parents should make it clear that a custody arrangement is not going to change simply because the child wants less responsibility and oversight. As much as possible, parents need to be together on an approach to discipline (ex., bedtimes, screen time, chores, homework) and support one another. This would be important even if separation and divorce were not part of the picture.

Spending Time Together

Unless there are safety issues, every effort should be made to have children spend adequately balanced time with the non-custodial parent and custodial parent. Try to also total it between structured, more intense activity and non-structured, laid-back freedom. Instead of a restaurant meal, it might be a better idea to go grocery shopping together and cook the meal at home, even if cooking abilities are low-level. Instead of constantly being on the go, parent and child might want to spend a more relaxing evening playing a game both enjoy or just watching a favorite TV program together—unless you're using television as a cop-out for talking and interaction with the child.

Take time to attend school and extracurricular events, and make sure that you don't ruin an event by displaying any hostility toward one another. Children of divorce often comment on how sad they feel when only one parent attends a school play or comes to a sports activity—even if only one attended before the divorce.

If your children are interested, invite them to share in your hobbies. Learn more about theirs or find something new that you can take up together like cooking, tennis, photography, or collecting and trading comic books.

Parents should remember that court-appointed visiting rights are usually only minimal for supporting continuing contact for a non-custodial parent. Seeing children only several times a year or occasionally on weekends and holidays may lead to difficulty in knowing what your children's changing interests are or what to do with them during a visitation.

I want to stress one more very important factor here: Be reliable. If you tell your children that you will be seeing them at a particular time, be there. Don't promise you'll be doing things with them and then not follow through. The best thing that you can do for them is to make whatever sacrifices necessary to keep your promises to them, to stay close to them, and to remain as involved as possible in their everyday lives.

The bottom line is that you stay involved in your children's life. Show an interest in how they spend their days. Get to know their friends. Find out what's going on in school. Be there for them.

Needs and Wants

When parenting children in any situation, needs obviously should take natural precedence over wants. This is particularly true if the parent who has physical custody and has not been employed prior to the breakup or has limited education or job experience. The result can be a family in financial straits.

As you know, there are a number of factors on which the courts decide custody, and child support is usually awarded to the custodial parent to help with the expenses of rearing the child. If you are a parent who is paying child support, this can seem like a burden—particularly if you are remarried and have begun a new family. Also, you could be dissatisfied with pressure to pay more or have the feeling that your ex-spouse is using the money for other purposes. Pay what is fair and mandated by the court (more when you can), and don't be critical about how it's being spent by the custodial parent unless your child is not receiving adequate necessities. If you have a poor relationship with your child's custodial parent, you may experience a situation where seeing your children depends on whether or not you pay child custody payments on time. If so, keep in mind that your children need both your emotional and financial support until they become independent. Find a way to make sure they have that.

As children grow, they (or their parents) may have different needs with respect to physical custody. In some cases, it would be truly beneficial to reevaluate a prior custody decision because of changing needs of various family members. Perhaps the custodial parent needs a rest from parenting responsibility or needs to put more energy into a career than earlier. Children grow older and may feel that one parent is better able to fulfill their needs at a particular time. For example, when children become adolescents and are struggling to organize their own identities, it is helpful for them to be with their same-sex parent. This can be particularly tough on the current custodial parent who may view children as disloyal or ungrateful for past care. If they'd be in favor of a change, children should not be caught in these kinds of loyalty binds with parents or made to suffer guilt. Also, children can only get to know their parents intimately when they live with that parent on a daily basis, watching attitudes, values, and coping skills being put into practice. For these reasons, custodial parents need to be considerate of the child's developing needs and periodically reassess whether or not they are providing the best possible environment for their children. That's true, unselfish love for a child.

Parent/Child Alienation

The concept of "parent alienation" or "child alienation" continues to be controversial, but there is little doubt that it exists. It occurs in family systems where a child develops and expresses an unreasonably strong dislike of one of the parents that doesn't seem to be justified. This animosity that is created between a parent and child is usually fueled by a parent who continues to feel bitter over the divorce. There may be unresolved anger about an affair that led to the divorce, financial arrangements that seem unfair, or lingering resentment about any number of issues. Eventually, the problem takes on a life of its own where all the players—parents and children—contribute to the situation in some way and keep it going.[101]

Richard Warshak[102] has written extensively over time about the fact that divorce does not always damage children. But when children are caught in the crossfire of their parents' hostility, it usually does. His studies of parent and child alienation, which he has labeled "divorce poison," resulted in his not seeing parents reject their children but about children who would have nothing to do with a parent who had always been devoted to them. He describes various levels of alienation. The worst is when the parent/child relationship is totally severed over time and where the alienated parents are not welcome at graduation ceremonies, are excluded from weddings, and have no contact with their grandchildren. Most cases of alienation, although not that severe, do result in the following:

- Tainted relationships between parents and children
- More conflict in the child's relationship with both parents and continued conflict between parents
- Less information flow between parents and among parents and children
- More withdrawal and reluctance of children to discuss their thoughts and feelings
- Children who have less respect for their parents' authority and less affection for their parents
- Troubling conflicts in children's feelings about their parents and about themselves
- Bad-mouthing, bashing, and brainwashing relative to grandparents and diminishing relationships

Okay—but what to do when you have genuinely tried to ward off or reverse the alienation that is coming from a hostile ex-spouse, and the situation continues to get worse? Consider this family:

Beth felt so betrayed by Kevin's affair that she took the children from Arizona back to Indiana, moving in with her mother. Following her divorce, and even after she remarried, she continually badmouthed Kevin to anyone who would listen, often in the earshot of her 7-year-old daughter and 5-year-old son. Prior to visitations, she would inject the children with "sympathetic laments" that she knew how hard it was to go to their dad's but that she would be thinking about them and missing them the whole time they were away. While her daughter and son were with their father, she continually emailed them and telephoned, whispering to them that she loved and missed them but that they didn't have much longer to go for the visit and to just "hang in there."

Over the next 10 years, her alienation tactics turned into true brainwashing, with the children coming to feel that their father couldn't really "love" anyone, including them, and that he was just demanding his time with them to "get back at" Beth and to control them. They became increasingly disrespectful to Kevin and his new partner Alma who had tried to be friendly and supportive during the children's visits. Nothing worked, and visitations became strained and ugly, not only with Kevin and Alma but also the children's paternal grandparents. Finally, the children's continued resistance, their mother's intensive efforts to undermine their father, expensive court visits, discouraging counseling sessions, and negative behavior wore Kevin down and visits were discontinued altogether. Today, Kevin makes little effort to be in contact with his children, and the possibility of any future connections looks bleak. "He deserves it," says Beth. "He got what he deserved!"

Dr. Richard Gardner,[103] who was the first professional to define parent and child alienation, doesn't mince words in his popular texts, *The Boys and Girls Book about Divorce*, *The Parents Book about Divorce*, and *The Parent Alienation Syndrome: A guide for Mental Health and Legal Professionals*. He is brutally honest about what can happen following divorce when parents drift into neglectful and unhealthy behaviors, both with each other and with their children. It can be difficult to convince parents like Beth about the harm she is doing by continuing to alienate her children. Although she has been advised often that her narcissism, unresolved anger, and inability to get on with a healthier future seems directed toward hurting Kevin, she is, in fact, being unfair to her son and daughter, destructive, and even psychologically abusive. Yet, she is unable to change her behavior.

The outcomes are predictable and often include:

- Unwarranted refusal of visitations and a parent's lack of access to the child

- Non-payment of child support in retaliation for issues related to visitation, causing increased hostility and financial issues

- Breakdown in the attachment and alignment between the alienated parent and children

- Overall family dysfunction

- Undermining of one parent by another

- Children learning to be manipulative and to view adult relationships in an unhealthy way

- Continued unhappiness and lack of stability and security

Family therapy may be helpful in situations like these but only if there is eventual acknowledgement by family members of the role each is playing, an understanding of how it is ultimately harmful to all concerned, and discontinued alienation behavior. Once alienation has taken root, it's difficult to turn around.

Predictably, this will be a difficult time for you. While your children need you more than ever, you may find yourself emotionally unavailable or feel that family life as you knew it can never be happy again. Keep in mind the old adage that bad times have endings as well as beginnings and that you will eventually feel a restoration of equilibrium for you and your children. An important factor in how quickly that happens is to understand that though your relationship with your partner is over, your children will still need time and positive relationships with both of you. One of the most important things I have learned through studies of divorced families is that children who have frequent and regular contacts with both parents fare much better after divorce. They also benefit when they can continue to have contact with friends and relatives of both parents. This calls for both parents to stress the good points about the other one, to avoid name calling, or blaming the other parent for problems.

Richard Victor, an Oakland County, Michigan lawyer, tells the story of the child who finished a phone call with his mother who was the non-custodial parent. "I tried to tell Mom that I'm getting a Scout award next week, but she said that she couldn't come because she was getting an award herself that night at work," whined the seven-year-old to his father.

The father, who felt that his ex-wife frequently put her work before the welfare of her children, was tempted to share his feelings and side in with his son's dissatisfaction. However, because he was convinced that his son needed to have as positive an attitude as possible toward his mother, the father suggested, "I know how disappointed your mom has to be. She'll feel pretty awful not to be there. I also know that she would have liked to have you there to see *her* get her award. Lots of good things are happening all at the same time! Why don't we call up and order some flowers for her? What do you think we should put on the card?" The father said that the expense of the flowers was worth seeing his son light up, losing his own disappointment as he refocused on the surprise for his mother—a good lesson for the future.

Remember that your children are depending on both you and your ex-spouse to protect them as much as possible as you deal with all the ups and downs your divorce brings. You can only shield your children if you resolve to put them first. Somehow, you need to find the strength to do that—to provide the love, guidance, and stability they need now more than ever. They will observe first-hand how adults they love can come through a series of difficult personal challenges and still emerge hopeful about the future—with their integrity and self-esteem intact.

I know that it is not the event of the divorce itself that harms a child, but rather the continued conflict between parents. The good news is that, through cooperative efforts, parents can prevent or minimize the negative impact of divorce on their children. To the extent that they can learn to set aside their own conflicts and restructure their family relationships in a new and healthy way, the future for their children can be happier and more secure.

New Family Formations

Seventy-five percent of divorced spouses remarry. Given the fact that most divorces occur roughly six or seven years after a first marriage, chances are good that young parents who remarry will have biological children. According to the U.S. Census, more than 50 percent of all children are now living with one biological parent and that parent's partner.[104]

The eventual remarriage of either one of you has the potential to create an entirely new set of issues that usually crop up at one time or another in a blended family. There may be weakened sexual taboos, different life histories and lifestyles, matters of loyalty and affection, and difficulty in deciphering roles. Also, the competition between natural parents and stepparents and between stepsiblings may rear its head.[105]

Whether or not the stepchildren will be living with you on a full-time basis, it will take time to get to know each other, to become comfortable with one another, and to establish ways of interacting on a daily basis. Also, because there are usually the other biological parents in the lives of all the children involved in the newly blended family, it will be critical to develop relationships that are characterized by dignity and respect—both for the sanity of the adults and the well-being of the children.

When there are going to be stepsiblings living together, they can become competitive with one another, fighting verbally and physically for years, with conflict continuing even into adulthood. Or they can become good friends, with devotion that lasts a lifetime. Much will depend on human chemistry, personalities, temperaments, and age differences. But more will depend on how you and your spouse handle any concerns that involve fairness in splitting up chores, rivalry, space, sharing, feelings of favoritism, activities, and disputes.

The bottom line is that you will want to tread carefully not to undermine one another or create unhealthy alliances. Never begin to think that you and your new spouse will not have to work hard at the restructuring involved in a step-parenting situation. You'd get off on the wrong foot if you have expectations that your new family will mirror the Brady Bunch and that respect, love, and changes will automatically fall into place. They won't. Following is a listing of some of the work that may be ahead of you and your new spouse when blending families:[106]

- Continuing to put your relationship first and providing needed support for one another
- Moving in together and sharing space
- Bonding with your new stepchildren. Listen but don't tell the child you know how he/she feels. You don't.
- Establishing what a stepchild will be calling you.
- Being creative with other biological parents about sharing holidays
- How to handle old traditions and establish new ones
- Establishing guidelines for handling discipline issues and commonalities with the other biological parents
- Working together on behavioral issues
- Dealing with extended families
- Watching for any violations of sexual taboos between reblended family members
- The potential impact of having children of your own
- Handling legal and financial matters fairly and honestly[107]

If you find yourself in the situation where you are frustrated or troubled about any of the above, there are a number of good publications on the market about coping with becoming a stepparent and stepfamily. Be aware of your own feelings and if you need to talk, find a trusted friend, therapist, or support group in your community. Do this *before* you become overly stressed or find that the situation is becoming overwhelming and possibly leading to more disruption.

As in all families—biological or blended - many of the problems you may experience in the future will be unforeseen and will arise over the course of time. The best and only way to deal with these is to forestall negative judgments, include everyone involved in open communication and decision making, respect everyone's feelings, and do the best you can to protect the viability of all relationships concerned.

Questions Parents Ask

Q: How can I enforce drop-off and pick-up times?

A: One thing to remember is that we can never control another person. That person must want to be cooperative and keep things running smoothly for the sake of his or her children. The best way to ensure that is not to "enforce," but to treat the other person with respect at all times, not being overly critical, acting responsibly yourself, and being as flexible as possible so that molehills don't become mountains. Courts cannot mandate that parents be civil or cooperative toward one another. However, when parents cannot resolve hostility and use it to irritate an ex-spouse whenever they have contact with one another, they and their children will continue to suffer. Choosing to remain unhappy in order to get back at another person is unhealthy and is predictable of poor adjustment for children as well. You can depend on it.

Q: How can I help my kids control their anger and emotions?

A: While you must acknowledge your children's negative emotions, you must also forbid destructive behavior. For example, you need to say, "It's all right to be angry. It's not okay to hit or call people names or break things." Often, just having you acknowledge out loud that you recognize how angry your child is can go a long way to satisfying his/her emotional needs. To help children control their anger and emotions, keep in mind the following principles:

1. Children's emotions are real and legitimate to them.

2. There are no right or wrong emotions. All feelings stem from core emotions, which occur naturally.

3. Children are not adept at regulating their emotions; nor can they simply change their emotions on command.

4. All emotions serve a useful function in children's lives.

Refer back to Chapter 2 to review some of the skills that are suggested for adults to promote children's understanding and communication about emotions. Use stories and books (ex. *Dinosaur's Divorce);* prompt them to describe how they feel and help them to sort out mixed emotions about the situation. For strong emotions, acknowledge them: "You're really angry. I see that." Comfort children when they are sad or afraid: "Sometimes people feel better when they talk about their feelings. If you want to talk, I'm here to listen." Redefine events when they have misinterpreted other people's actions or intents. Point out facts that they may have overlooked: "You thought your dad didn't show up because he doesn't care. He did call and apologize and try to reschedule with you." Anticipate new situations that might cause them to feel insecure, such as further changes. Teach them self-regulating strategies they can use to manage their emotions more effectively, such as talking to themselves ("I miss my mom, but just because I can't live with her doesn't mean she doesn't love me or has forgotten about me." "I can stay calm. I don't have to hit or yell." "I 'm sad (scared, mad, lonely), but I can handle this by taking some deep breaths, counting to 10, or by looking at a difficult situation in more optimistic terms (my mom and dad are getting a divorce, but I still get to see them both often). Be careful about trying to diffuse their emotions too quickly ("Don't be a baby." "Snap out of it.") or telling them "It'll be the same. You'll see...." when it won't be.

When children are acting out in disrespectful ways, try to determine what they really want. For example, "You want to live with your dad, so you're refusing to cooperate with me. Not doing what I've asked you to do is not acceptable (here, a change in tone of voice is indicated) and won't be tolerated! I'm here to help you. We need to talk more about what *really* has you so upset."

One thing that parents must examine when their children remain angry and tremendously sad about the divorce is how they are behaving toward each other. If they continue to argue and fight in front of their children, they heighten their children's sense of insecurity. Remember that every time you fight in front of your children or badmouth your ex-partner, you tear them apart, make them feel more and more alone, and more filled with rage and anger.

Q: What about custodial or non-custodial parents who move away?

A: Increasing the distance between parent and a dependent child is *not* a good decision and should be avoided at all costs. All evidence weighs against it. It can never be a fair decision and unless there are safety reasons, there is nothing that indicates that both parents should have any *less* right or *greater* right to participate in the rearing of their children. If you are a non-custodial parent, you will want to maintain your attachment to your children and have the right to contest a custodial parents' move out of state and should do so in court if necessary. Custodial parents who wish to move out of state to pursue employment opportunities or other relationships are making personal choices that are not in the best interest of their children. Non-custodial parents who move far distances from their children with the belief that they can make up for it by summer visits should know that their choice is also a poor one, particularly as children get older and do not want to leave their friends, activities, and neighborhood for visitations. The best thing that parents can do for their children is to make whatever sacrifices necessary to stay close to them and as involved as possible in their everyday life.

Q: Is it ever a good idea to split up brothers and sisters?

A: No. They deserve to grow up knowing one another and should never be treated as property to "divvy up" after a divorce. Brothers and sisters can provide a great deal of support to one another during and following their parents' divorce. Splitting them up would only serve to fracture the family even further and should not be considered an option. When children are adolescents, however, it may be that they request a change of custody. If there are substantial reasons why this should be done, it may be considered. However, in most cases, despite the fact that a lot of quarreling may go on between children, they are still one another's best friends when one truly needs a friend. They need to have daily access to one another.

Q: How do you ensure that your ex-spouse will stay involved with the kids?

A: The more access a parent has to a child—without hassles from the custodial parent—the more likely that parent is to stay involved in the child's life. Keep the other parent informed about the child's friends, school activities, needs and interests. Make sure the child acknowledges the non-custodial parent's birthday and shares holiday celebrations with him or her. Remain connected with the non-custodial parent's family, encouraging children to visit with grandparents, cousins, and relatives. Allow your child to talk freely about the other parent and be sure the child has pictures of the other parent in his or her room. Help the child stay in touch as much as possible through technology and actual visits.

If a parent does abandon a child or if there are only sporadic visits or contacts, be careful about being critical. Remember that children fare better when they have a good opinion of both parents. Acknowledge your child's disappointment when it is expressed. You can say, "Sometimes when people find things too hurtful, they just avoid it. Sometimes, adults become involved in their own problems…and that might be what's happening with your (mother, dad)." Assure your child that you will always be there, no matter what. One conversation about this may not be enough.

Red Flags

1. Financial decisions are unfair, leaving the custodial parent struggling to supply true necessities for children.

2. One parent is assuming most or all of the responsibility for raising the children.

3. Children rarely see the non-custodial parent or are not allowed to see the extended family of the non-custodial parent.

4. Children feel caught in a loyalty bind and are unable to say anything positive about the other parent or other parent's "new" family.

5. Parents continue to be hostile toward one another, arguing in front of their children and in public places. There is parent alienation operating.

6. Parents are frequently in and out of court and cannot work through disagreements with one another without legal counsel.

7. The non-custodial parent is not paying court-mandated child support.

8. Parents in a new relationship exhibit overt sexual behavior in front of children.

9. One parent is stalking, threatening, or abusive toward the other one; an ex-spouse has to obtain a restraining order; there is suspected sexual, psychological, or physical abuse of children.

10. After a two-year period beyond the divorce, the family still lacks stability and has not restructured in a healthy way.

What's in Your Parenting Toolkit?

1. So that your children don't think an impending divorce is their fault, tell them early in the process that separation and divorce are adult problems to be worked out and not their fault in any way.

2. As much as possible, tell your children what the future means for them in terms of where they will be living, any changes that are necessary, how often they'll be able to see the non-custodial parent, and so on. Answer their questions honestly but without adding to their distress.

3. If you do not have shared or physical custody, find a way to maintain a consistent, continuous relationship with your children and interest in what they're doing.

4. Let your child's teacher and school know what's going on.

5. Do not speak negatively about, cut down the other parent, or undermine that parent. It will only harm your child's sense of security and self-esteem.

6. Maintain as much consistency for your child as possible in terms of housing, school, friends, relationships with extended family members, and extra-curricular activities.

7. If you are a non-custodial parent, show up when you say you're going to and pay child support on schedule. Don't try to win your child over by expensive gifts or excessive entertainment.

8. Work with the other parent to maintain a similar approach to discipline, expectations for behavior (ex. completion of homework). Do not allow children to pit one parent against another or be manipulative.

9. Do not use your child as a counselor. If you need to discharge feelings or talk about "the situation," talk with a friend or a professional.

10. Understand that while your relationship with your ex-spouse has ended, your parenting responsibilities must continue and, unless there are problems with safety it's best if you carry them out together.

Conclusion

Children *can* learn to be happy and feel secure again after their parents' divorce. This depends, of course, on how seriously their parents take their co-parenting responsibilities afterwards and whether or not they can put aside their own differences for their children's sake. This calls for cooperation and compromise by both ex-spouses, active stress management by parents, and a commitment by both to restructure the family into a new, healthy, and well-functioning unit.

Endnotes

1. Kostelnik, M. J., Soderman, A. K., Whiren, A. P. & Rupiper, M. L. (2018). *Guiding Children's Social Development & Learning: Theory and Skills*. Boston, MA: Cengage Learning.

2. See Kostelnik, et al., 2018.

3. See Kostelnik, et al., 2018.

4. Bob Seeger and Erik Clapton. Harry Chapin's *The Cat's in the Cradle*.

5. Personal conversation with Marvin H. McKinney, Senior Consultant, Michigan State University and Program Director for Youth Programs at the W. K. Kellogg Foundation in Battle Creek, MI.

6. Elkind, D. (2006). *Miseducation: Preschoolers at Risk*. Cambridge, MA: Da Capo Press

7. Gottman, J. & Silver, N. (2015). *The Seven Principles for Making Marriage Work*. New York: Random House

8. Turecki, T. & Tonner, L. (2000). *The Difficult Child*. (New York: Bantam Books.

9. See Turecki et al. (2000), p. 187

10. Bronfenbrenner, B. (1972). *Two Worlds of Childhood: U.S. and U.S.S.R.* New York: Simon and Schuster.

11. Aamodt, S. & Sam Wang (2012). *Welcome to Your Child's Brain*. New York: Bloomsbury.

12. See Kostelnik et al. (2018).

13. Erik H. Erikson (1963). *Childhood and Society*. New York: W. W. Norton & Company.

14. See Kostelnik et al. (2018), pp. 148-149.

15. See Kostelnik et al. (2018), pp. 148-149.

16. Reiss, H. & Neporent, L. (2018). *The Empathy Effect: Seven Neuroscience-Based Keys for Transforming the Way We Live, Love, Work and Connect across Differences.* Boulder, CO: Sounds True.

17. Goleman, D. (2007). *Social Intelligence: The New Science of Human Relationships.* New York: Bantam Dell.

18. Churchland, P. (2019). *Conscience: The Origins of Moral Intuition.* New York: W. W, Norton.

19. Kostelnik, M. J., Soderman, A. K. Whiren, A. P. & Rupiper, M. L. (2019). *Developmentally Appropriate Curriculum: Best Practices in Early Childhood Education.* Boston: Pearson.

20. Delman, M. (2018). *Your Kid's Gonna Be Okay: Building the Executive Function Skills Your Child Needs in the Age of Attention* (Kindle Edition).

21. Lantieri, L. & Goleman, D. (2014). *Building Emotional Intelligence: Practices to Cultivate Inner Resilience in Children.* Boulder, CO: Sounds True, Inc.

22. Elias, M. J. & Arnold, H. A. (2006). *The Educator's Guide to Academic Achievement.* Thousand Oaks, CA: Corwin Press.

23. Strosnider, R. & Sharpel, V. (2019). *The Executive Function Guidebook: Strategies to Help All Students Achieve Success.* Thousand Oaks, CA: Corwin Press.

24. Cloniger, C. R., Cloniger, K. M., Zwir, I. & Keltikangas-Jarvinen, L. (November 2019). The complex genetics and biology of human temperament: A review of traditional concepts in relation to new molecular findings, *Transitional Psychiatry,* 9, no 290.

25. Thomas, A., Chess, S. & Korn, S. J. (1982). The reality of difficult temperament, *Merrill-Palmer Quarterly,* 28 (1) 1-20.

26. Stephens, K. (2007). Strategies for parenting children with difficult temperament, Parenting Exchange. www.ParentingExchange.com.

27. See Kostelnik et al., (2018), p. 160.

28. Ginsburg, K. R. (2015). *Building Resilience in Children and Teens: Giving Kids Roots and Wings, 3rd Ed.* Elk Grove Village, IL: American Academy of Pediatrics, 201, p. 4.

29. See Kostelnik et al., (2018), p. 174.

30. Masten, A. S. (2014). *Ordinary Magic: Resilience in Development.* New York: Guildford Press.

31. See Kostelnik et al., (2018).

32. Seligman, M. E. P. (2018). *The Hope Circuit: A Psychologist's Journey from Helplessness to Optimism.* New York: Hachette Book Group.

33. See Ginsburg (2015), p. 375.

34. See Seligman (2018).

35. Schmitt, B. M.D. (2020). Sibling Rivalry toward a Newborn. PediaClinic.com,

36. See Ginsburg (2015).

37. Robertson, N. Morrisey, A. and Rouse, E. (February 2018). *Play-based learning can set your child up for success at school and beyond.* The Conversation.com

38. Quote from Kay Redfield Jamison, American clinical psychologist and writer, Professor at Johns Hopkins University School of Medicine.

39. Kostelnik et al., (2018), p. 182.

40. Gonzalez-Mena, J. & Eyer, D. W. (2020). *Infants, Toddlers, and Caregivers: A Curriculum of Respectful, Responsive, Relationship Based Care and Education, 10th Ed.* New York: McGraw Hill.

41. Decker, C. (2015). *Child Development: Early Stages through Age 12, 8th Ed.* Goodheart-Willcox.

42. Frances Ilg and Louise Bates Ames published a number of books on children's development at each year of age (see Amazon listings).

43. Kostelnik et al., (2018), p. 185.

44. Hearron, P. F. & Hildebrand, V. P. (2012). *Guiding Young Children, 9th Ed.* Boston: Pearson.

45. Padilla-Walker, L. M. & Carlo, G., Eds. (2014). *Prosocial Development.* New York: Oxford University.

46. Kostelnik et al., (2018), p. 407.

47. Kostelnik, et al., (2018), p. 233.

48. Bagwell, C. L. (2013). *Friendships in Childhood & Adolescence.* New York: The Guilford Press.

49. Kostelnik et al., (2018), p. 244.

50. Kostelnik et al., (2018), pp 372-373.

51. Kaiser, B. & Rasminsky, J. S. (2016). *Challenging. Behavior in Young Children: Understanding, Preventing, & Responding Effectively, 4th Ed.* Boston: Pearson.

52. Hinduja, S. & Patchin, J. W. (2016). *Bullying Today.* Thousand Oaks, CA: Corwin.

53. Burnhan, J. J. & Wright, V. H. (2012). Cyberbullying: What Middle School Students Want You to Know, *Alabama Counseling Association Journal,* 38 (1), 1-12.

54. Patchin, J. W. & Hinduja, S. (2010). *Words Wound: Delete Cyberbullying and Make Kindness Go Viral.* Minneapolis, MN: Free Spirit Publishers.

55. Yellend, N. J. (2010). New technologies, playful experiences, and multimodal learning, In Berson, I. R. & Berson, M. J. (2010). *High Tech Tots: Children in a Digital World,* Charlotte, NC: Information Age Publishing

56. Moreno, M. A., Chassiakos, Y. R., & Cross, C., (November 2016). Media Use in School-Age Children and Adolescents, Pediatrics, 138 (5) e20162592.

57. Livingstone, S. & Blum-Ross, A. (2020). *Parenting for a Digital Future. How Hopes and Fears about Technology Shape Children's Lives.* New York: Oxford University Press.

58. Vasquez, V. M. & Felderman, C. B. (2012). *Technology and Critical Literacy in Early Childhood.* New York: Routledge

59. See Livingstone & Blum-Ross (2020).

60. Rothfield-Kirschner, L. (2019). *How We Got Cyber Smart: A Book about How to Stay Safe Online* (Kindle Edition). Rembrandt Street Publishing.

61. Azevedo, F. (2020). *How to Defend against Cyberbullies and Trolls: The Inner Working of the Internet for Parents.* Kindle Edition.

62. Moreno, M. A., Chassiakos, Y. R., & Cross, C., (November 2016). Media Use in School-Age Children and Adolescents, *Pediatrics*, 138.

63. Dwight, E. (2019). Here's how parents can keep kids safe online without spying, *All the MOMS.* Downloaded on 7/24/20.

64. See App to keep parents and educators updated on social media: SmartSocial.com.

65. Batshaw, M. L., Roizen, N. & Pellegrino, L. (2019). *Children with Disabilities, 8th Ed.* Baltimore: Paul H. Brookes Publishing Co

66. See Kostelnik et al. (2018).

67. Sandfort, T. G. M. & Rademakers, J. (2013). *Childhood Sexuality: Normal Sexual Behavior and Development.* New York: Routledge.

68. American Academy of Pediatrics (April 2019). What's normal, What's not? Sexual Behavior Problems in Young Children. Healthychildren.org.

69. See Kostelnik et al. (2018).

70. Pickering, R. (2020). *A Modern Approach to the Birds & the Bees: A Parent's Comprehensive Guide to Talking about Sexuality.* Mango.

71. LeVay, S. (2016). *Gay, Straight, and the Reason Why: The Science of Sexual Orientation, 2nd Ed.* New York: Oxford.

72. Freeman, Y. S., Freeman, D. E. Ramirez, R. (2008). *Diverse Learners in the Mainstream Classroom.* Portsmouth, NH: Heinemann.

73. Freeman et al., (2008).

74. Derman-Sparks, L. & Edwards, J. O. (2020). *Anti–Bias Education for Young Children and Ourselves.* Washington, DC: National Association for the Education of Young Children

75. American Psychiatric Association (2013). *Diagnostic and Statistical Manual of Mental Disorders, 5th Ed.* (DSM-5) Author.

76. Fonseca, C. (2015). *Raising the Shy Child.* Waco, TX: Prufrock Publishing, p. 8.

77. Fonseca, C. (2015), pp. 8-9.

78. Teetsel, R. N., Ginsburg, G. S., & Drake, K. L. (2014). Anxiety-promoting parenting behaviors: A comparison of anxious mothers and fathers. *Child Psychiatry & Human Development*, 45, 133-142.

79. See Fonseca, C. (2015), p. 117.

80. See Fonseca, (2015).

81. Renzulli, J. S. & Reis, S. M. (1997). The Schoolwide Enrichment Model, 2nd Ed. Mansfield, OH: Creative Learning Press, 5-14.

82 Figure 4.1: 3-ring Venn diagram of Renzulli's model. Renzulli Learning.com

83. Reid, C. & Romanoff, B. (September 1997). Using multiple intelligence theory to identify gifted children, *Educational Leadership,* 55 (1), 71-74.

84 Sternberg, R. (1984). *Beyond IQ: A Triarchic Theory of Human. Intelligence.* New York: Cambridge University Press.

85. Sternberg, R. (2019). *Human Intelligence: An Introduction.* New York: Cambridge University Press.

86. Kostelnik, M. J., Soderman, A. K., Whiren, A. P. & Rupiper, M. L. (2019). *Developmentally Appropriate Curriculum*. Boston: Pearson, p. 336.

87. Kostelnik et al. (2018), p. 445.

88. Ormrod, J. E., Anderman, E. M. & Anderman, L. H. (2019). *Educational Psychology: Developing Learners*. Boston: Pearson.

89. Gardner, H. (2012). *Summary: Five minds for the future*. Amazon Digital Services.

90. See Gardner (2012).

91. See Batshaw et al. (2019), p. 587.

92. Pickering, R. (2020). *A Modern Approach to the Birds & the Bees: A Parent's Comprehensive Guide to Talking about Sexuality*. Mango.

93. Bering, J. (July 2012). Is your child gay? *Scientific American*, 23 (3), 50-53.

94. See Batshaw et al. (2019).

97. See Batshaw (2019), p. 131.

96. Trail, B. (2011). *Twice Exceptional Gifted Children: Understanding, Teaching, and Counseling Gifted Students*. Waco, TX: Prufrock Press, Inc.

97. Soderman, A. K., Chhikara, S., Hsiu-Ching, C. & Kuo, E. (October 1999). Gender differences that affect emerging literacy in first grade children: U. S., India, and Taiwan, *International Journal of Early Childhood*, 31 (2), 9-16.

98. Van Viersen, S., Kroesbergen, E. H., Slot, E. M., & de Bree, E. H. (Mar-Apr 2016). High reading skills mask dyslexia in gifted children, *Journal of Learning Disabilities*, 49 (2), 189-99.

99. Joe DiMaggio, Jr. in a 1982 interview on Larry King Live.

100. Soderman, A. K., Eveland, T. & Ellard, M..(2000). *In Your Child's Best Interest: A Guide for Divorcing Parents*. E. Lansing, MI: Michigan State University Extension.

101. Haines, J., Matthewson, M. & Turnbull, M. (2019). *Understanding and Managing Parental Alienation: A Guide to Assessment and Intervention.* New York: Routledge

102. Warshak, R. A. (2015). *Divorce Poison: How to Protect Your Family from Bad Mouthing and Brainwashing.* Tantor Audio; MP3 - Unabridged CD edition. Also available in paperback, 2010.

103. Gardner, R. (1987). The Parent Alienation Syndrome and the Differentiation between Fabricated and Genuine Child Sex Abuse. *Creative Therapeutics.*

104. Gaspard, G. (2020). *The Remarriage Manual: How to Make Everything Better the Second Time Around.* Available on Kindle only, Sounds True.

105. See Kostelnik et al. (2018).

106. Wallerstein, J. S. & and Blakeslee, S. (2018). *Second Chances: Men, Women and Children, A Decade after Divorce.* nwallerstein@salud.unm.edu.

107. See www.stepfam.org.

Acknowledgements

I want to express my sincere gratitude to my colleagues, Marjorie J. Kostelnik, Alice P. Whiren, Michele L. Rupiper, Kara Gregory, and Laura Stein. Our friendship and work together over the years to create the nine editions of *Children's Social Development and Learning* (Cengage Learning, 2018) served ultimately as the primary knowledge base for *A Parenting Toolkit*. While our purpose has been primarily to train early childhood educators with the suggestions and skill sets described herein, we also shared the same information in newsletters and workshops with multitudes of parents in local, national, and international settings. I am grateful to those parents for what they taught us in our many interactive discussions. I also want to acknowledge collaboration with Thomas S. Eveland, Circuit Court Judge, Eaton County, Michigan, and Mona J. Ellard, former Eaton County Extension Director in creating SMILE, a program for divorcing parents with dependent children. I drew on our work extensively for the contents of Chapter 5. My own three children certainly kept me grounded and able to measure the true worth and substance of what I have chosen to share in these pages.

Effective strategies to guide and care for young children should not differ significantly, whether applied by educators or by parents. Admittedly, what does vary is that the time shared by teachers and children (although highly important) is relatively limited, as is the strength of the bonding and rapport that develops. Parent and child unions, with the kind of interpersonal and psychological attachments fostered as a result, are much more critical in a child's development. Whether they are mostly positive or mostly negative, they last forever.

Thank you again to Kelly Nielsen at Studio 92 for his skilled attention to detail, thoughtful commentary, and meticulous editing that allowed me to bring this effort to completion.

Index

www.ingramcontent.com/pod-product-compliance
Lightning Source LLC
Chambersburg PA
CBHW071415150726
48000CB00001B/334